BIBLE EPITAPHS

BIBLE EPITAPHS

CLARENCE EDWARD MACARTNEY

BAKER BOOK HOUSE
Grand Rapids, Michigan

Reprinted 1974 by Baker Book House
with the permission of Abingdon Press
ISBN: 0-8010-5963-1

PHOTOLITHOPRINTED BY CUSHING - MALLOY, INC.
ANN ARBOR, MICHIGAN, UNITED STATES OF AMERICA
1974

FOREWORD

As the title suggests, this volume is made up of sermons on Bible Epitaphs. The Bible has an incomparable and inimitable way of etching its personalities and summing up their character. What could surpass its dismissal of Gehazi, "A leper as white as snow"? Or its farewell to Herod, "He was eaten of worms"? Or the Gospel's sigh over the Rich Young Ruler, "He went away sorrowful"? Or the thumbnail biography of Jabez, "He was more honorable than his brethren"? Or the final verdict as to Judas, "He went to his own place"?

Bible biography treated in this way affords an impressive, and somewhat unique, mode of preaching. I have taken up just a few of the striking epitaphs of the Bible. The door is wide open for other preachers who care to enter this chamber of instruction and inspiration.

CLARENCE EDWARD MACARTNEY.

CONTENTS

ABNER

I

"Died Abner as a fool dieth"

II Samuel 3: 33

LIFE is the great teacher. That is why biography is the greatest literature. The Bible is the greatest biographer, and, therefore, the greatest teacher.

What is recorded there of the lives of men is written for our admonition, "upon whom the ends of the ages are come." Not only what the men of the Bible say and do, not only the vivid and graphic descriptions of their actions and their impulses, but what is said of them after they are dead constitutes the great lessons of Bible biography. The sayings with which we shall deal in this series of sermons, and which I have called Bible Epitaphs, are what is said in the Bible of seventeen of its characters, some of them very well known and some not so familiar. These epitaphs are brief, pungent, sometimes pathetic utterances which not only sum up the life and character, relate the deeds and describe the death of the person over whom they were spoken, but teach great and timeless truths. They are sign-boards of wisdom along the highway of life. Customs, fashions, and manners change, almost with the swift alternation of the seasons of the year, but the great principles of life remain the same.

We hear much of a youth emphasis today; what youth is capable of, what it can do to right the wrongs and heal the wounds of mankind, and the opportunities which stand before its gate. But today, as much as ever, perhaps more than ever, youth needs counsel, encouragement, warning, and inspiration. Therefore, we shall let these Bible Epitaphs speak to the soul of youth.

The first of these is the epitaph which David spoke over the body of the slain Abner, "Died Abner as a fool dieth."

The tragedy of Abner is an event which belongs to the sunset of the reign of King Saul and the morning of David's reign. Abner was the chief prince and leader of the forces and followers of King Saul's son, Ish-bosheth. There was long war between the house of David and the house of Saul, and in that war the house of Saul waxed weaker and weaker, but the house of David waxed stronger and stronger. The chief pillar and prop of the house of Saul was the able and vigorous Abner, the son of Ner. Although he had put Ish-bosheth on a rival throne, Abner had become weary of the senseless slaughter of the civil war, and once had said to the chief captain of David, Joab, "Shall the sword devour forever?" He was undoubtedly planning to swing his influence to the house of David, when an event took place which brought him to a quick decision. Ish-bosheth, who owed all to Abner, charged him with a dishonorable act in connection with the family of Saul. Outraged at this evidence of ingratitude, Abner at once opened negotiations with David. David, weary himself of the internecine strife, welcomed the proposals of Abner, and arrangements were made for the cessation of the war and the support of the throne of David in all parts of Israel.

But in these negotiations David had forgotten the bitter enmity of his chief captain, Joab, toward Abner. This enmity had its beginning on the day when Abner, unwillingly, and not without repeated warning and remonstrance, slew the light-footed brother of Joab, Asahel, who pursued him after one of the battles between the house of David and the house of Saul. When Joab heard that David had come to an understanding with Abner, he went to David and rebuked him openly, telling him that he had been fooled and deceived by Abner, who had no thought of giving up the war against him, but had entered into negotiations with him to learn of his resources and his purposes. After this arrogant and impudent rebuke of the king, Joab sent messengers to Abner inviting him, apparently in the name of the king, to return to Hebron for another conference. Nothing doubting, Abner returned at once. He was met at the gate by the crafty Joab, who, with an assumed cordiality and friendship, took him aside to talk with him in the shadow of the gate. But as they talked together, Joab suddenly drew his sword and slew him. Thus he avenged the death of Asahel, his brother.

The treacherous murder of Abner occasioned David the greatest humiliation and grief. With all his faults, David was ever a magnanimous man. Nothing could have been more repugnant to him than the wicked and cruel treachery of Joab. He gave orders throughout the kingdom for a public mourning for Abner, proclaiming that a prince and a great man had fallen that day in Israel. When Abner was buried, David followed his coffin to the place of burial, and standing by the grave he wept and lamented for Abner, saying, "Died Abner as a fool dieth."

This exclamation, the dirge sung by David over the grave of Abner, has been lifted out of its immediate historical association and has become a proverb of all time, meaning the death in character, in influence, or life itself, of one who might have lived a useful and honorable life. "Died Abner as a fool dieth."

There was much in the character of Abner which was unworthy; but we shall not go astray if we take David's estimate of him, a prince and a great man, at its face value. Certainly, he was a distinguished and useful man, and had just accomplished a notable service in going over to the house of David with his army and thus putting an end to the cruel and sanguinary civil war which had long been raging and had cost thousands of lives and filled the land with blood and desolation. Now, just at the climax of his great career, Abner is slain. He was not slain in battle, in open conflict with his foes. That is what David meant in his dirge when he said, "Thy hands were not bound, nor thy feet put into fetters." His shield and buckler were not on his arm; his sword was not drawn; but he fell needlessly, foolishly, slain by the crafty and cruel Joab. Therefore, he died as the fool dieth. He ought to have been on his guard, knowing the past record of Joab, and ready to defend himself; but he walked foolishly into the trap Joab had set for him, and, without a chance to defend himself, was cut down by the gate of Hebron.

"Died Abner as a fool dieth." The opportunities and the riches of life are still as great as ever; but still the same crafty, treacherous, implacable, and inexorable enemies lie in wait for the lives of men. Of those who perish, all we can say is what David said through his tears as he looked down on the body of the prince and great man who had fallen that day in Israel, "Died Abner as a fool dieth." Thus are men cheated and fooled out of life.

I. Character and Manhood

In the first place, men die, as to character and manhood, and when they have died, the words of David fit them, "Died Abner as a fool dieth." The good man heads the holy procession of mankind; all others fall in behind him. Therefore, it is a sad thing to see men or women in the morning of life self-wounded, mutilated, handicapped at the very start of life's long race and the very opening of life's hard battle. Alas, how easily and how quickly can pearls of character and integrity be cast before the swine of appetite and that which is holy given to the dogs.

The thing that the Bible emphasizes about this, and all kinds of sin, is the folly of it. The supreme fool is the sinner. There are many things which are taken from a man without his will or consent, and even against it—his health, his wealth, his friends, his station in life. But the possessions of the soul—truth, honor, virtue, faith—these are never taken away except with our consent; and wherever a man so consents, there the best that is within him dies as the fool dieth. When character and integrity are gone, what remains is bestial.

Abner was treacherously slain, for Joab talked with him in a cordial way and greeted him as a friend. But that false friendship was only a prelude to the fatal thrust of Joab's sword. Temptation always comes in the guise of friendship when it persuades a man to part with sacred possessions. So men are deceived into believing that what they do, or propose to do, what they yield or permit, lies in the path of happiness. As the apostle puts it, "Promising them liberty, while they themselves are bond-servants of corruption; for of whom a man is overcome, of the same is he also brought into bondage." Thus men die, in the best part of them, as the fool dieth. Of how many gifted, attractive, and even potentially great lives this is all that can be said. They threw themselves away—their life, their strength, their happiness—"Died Abner as a fool dieth." Therefore, hold fast that which thou hast. Make every sacrifice in behalf of the soul and its welfare. In the words of Housman, the Shropshire poet:

"If it chance your eye offend you,
  Pluck it out, lad, and be sound:
'Twill hurt, but here are salves to friend you,
  And many a balsam grows on ground.

And if your hand or foot offend you,
  Cut it off, lad, and be whole;
But play the man, stand up and end you,
  When your sickness is your soul."

II. The Man of Faith

Men can be slain also in their faith. Disaster can be wrought not only by false principles of living, by forsaking the standards of true conduct, but by the corruption or the abandonment of faith. Abner, let it be remembered, was slain by one who came to him under the guise of friendship. So under the guise of conferring a benefit, of offering liberty and emancipation, the tempter deceives the soul and takes away its faith in God; and when faith is gone, the noblest part in man has perished.

How quickly and easily this can be done. Just the stale jest of an Ingersoll or a Paine; a disparaging remark by a college professor; a hostile paragraph in a book or magazine; the ridicule of a friend; or an assent, even for a moment, to the solicitation of temptation, and the man of faith is mortally wounded. The highest is discarded; the holiest is defiled; and the noblest in man is sold for a trifle. When this happens, all that one can say is, "Died Abner as a fool dieth."

There is nothing to compare with the grandeur and beauty of the Christian faith. Like the rainbow, it touches heaven and earth; it speaks of a divine origin; it unfolds the path of duty from day to day; it comforts amid the sorrows of life and shows a divine purpose in our trials and adversities. It strengthens us in our temptations, and in the hour of death it whispers to our soul the words of immortal hope and eternal life. No; there is nothing to compare with the grandeur and beauty of Christian faith. Do not be cheated out of it. Hold fast that which thou hast, and let no man take thy crown.

judicial, and, in this case, unutterably sad, "He went to his own place."

Peter did not say Judas went to hell, but to "his own place." At a summer conference, I once heard a speaker refer to the French skeptic, Voltaire, in these words, "After Voltaire had been dead and damned for a century." It fell with a harsh and unpleasant sound upon the ear, not because of any sympathy with Voltaire's hostility to Christianity, but because it seemed both un-Christian and presumptuous that even the best among men should speak of even the worst among men in such terms. It is one thing to declare the whole Gospel of Christ and warn the impenitent of the danger of condemnation hereafter; but another thing to put one's self in the place of the supreme Judge and allot to one's fellow-beings their eternal destiny. How different, then, is the spirit of Peter when he comes to speak of Judas Iscariot. All that he says of him is this brief, yet solemn and searching word, "He went to his own place."

Whatever that place was, and we cannot think of it as a place of joy or peace, it was his own place that Judas had chosen. He had prepared for it, asked for it by the deeds of his life, and now he had entered into it. A solemn truth this, that we all choose our own place. As Judas built his house, so do we. The plan of it, the foundations, the furniture, the decorations—all are of our choosing and our de-

"O world, thou choosest not the better part;
  It is not wisdom to be only wise,
  And on the inward vision close the eyes;
But it is wisdom to believe the heart.
Columbus found a world and had no chart,
  Save one that faith deciphered in the skies.
  To trust the soul's invincible surmise
Was all his science, and his only art.

Our knowledge is a torch of smoky pine
  That lights the pathway but one step ahead,
  Across a void of mystery and dread.
Bid, then, the tender light of faith to shine
  By which alone the mortal heart is led
Unto the thinking of the thought divine."[1]

Live greatly and nobly because you live in faith and in obedience to the great laws which God has revealed for our welfare and our eternal happiness. Some loved their life so well and so selfishly that they lost it; but others lived so nobly, so Christlike, and so victoriously that by losing their life they gained it. When they died the world's verdict was that they died as the fool dieth. Now we know better; we know that they died wisely and triumphantly because they lived and died for God.

[1] George Santayana.

JUDAS

II

"That he might go to his own place"

Acts 1: 25

IN his essay on "Persons One Would Wish to Have Seen," William Hazlitt makes Charles Lamb say: "I would fain see the face of him who, having dipped his hand in the same dish with the Son of Man, could afterward betray Him. I have no conception of such a thing, nor have I ever seen any picture that gave me the least idea of it."

No picture, Leonardo's, or that by any other artist, will ever tell the whole secret of Judas. Always he will be the enigma among the Apostles. In a way, he is the most definitely classified among the Twelve. He is dismissed with strong statements in the Gospels, such as: "This he said . . . . because he was a thief, and had the bag"; "Satan entered into him"; "Judas, who betrayed Him." Yet, on the other side, how hard it is to conceive of what he did. His

call to the discipleship, his comp
Christ, his avarice, his treason, his re
cide, his predestination—all this, t
in the same man, makes Judas a great
here is one thing, at least, that is sai
that we can all understand—"He we
place."

The disciples, one hundred and twe
were met together in Jerusalem after
of their Lord. Peter, who presided, call
choose a successor to Judas. He rehe
tory of Judas, and how prophecy had
in his tragic life and death. Nevertheless
numbered with the disciples, and had obt
of their ministry. Peter then goes on t
circumstances of the death of Judas, a
that was given to the field in which he
Aceldama—the field of blood. Quoting
ninth Psalm as a warrant for their proce
instructs the disciples to choose from tw
have been put forward a successor to Jud

The remarkable thing about this addre
upon Judas is its noble restraint. He does
him as a thief, or a traitor, or a murderer, a
he was; nor does he say of him, as John
"Satan entered into him." But he takes a
well of Judas with this single phrase, one
a word of meaning in it; genuinely Christ

sign. Wherever the soul of Judas is tonight, he is in his own place.

Could it be possible to say to ourselves tonight anything that could be more arresting or searching than this? As you and I go through life we are preparing a place for ourselves. Every thought that passes swiftly through the chambers of the mind, every desire, every impulse, every word that escapes our lips, every secret and every public act, is a building of our final house and a choosing of our ultimate place. Both in this life and in the life to come, every man has a place which he chooses and creates for himself.

"The tissue of the life to be,
We weave with colors all our own;
And on the fields of destiny
We reap as we have sown."

I. The High Place to Which All Men Are Called

Every man is called to a high place in life and in destiny, and, therefore, for all men such a place is possible. Judas did not occupy, finally, the high place to which he was called; but, as Peter says, fell away from it by transgression. Judas was called to follow Christ, called to be an apostle, called to be one of those who were to lay the foundations of the glorious temple of the Christian Church. But from that place and office he fell away. He might have been remembered today as we remember Peter, or John, or Matthew, or St. Paul. Instead of that, whenever you pronounce the word Judas, you always add those four other sad words of the Gospels, "Who also betrayed him." Yet we must remember that one day Judas in the streets of Jerusalem, or along the highway, or by the Sea of Galilee, heard the voice of Jesus for the first time and was charmed by it. "Charmed to confess and follow on," Judas, one likes to think, was in the beginning a sincere and earnest follower of Christ. How sad and terrible, then, that other place which he finally chose in exchange for the place to which Christ had called him.

This is one of the great and stirring things about Christianity. It proclaims to man that there is a high place waiting for him and invites him to enter into it. When Saul, seeking his father's asses, came to inquire of the man of God, Samuel, in the town of Zuph, Samuel told him that his father's lost asses had been found. He was not to think any more about them, for something greater was now in view. The throne of Israel had been chosen for him. "For whom is all that is desirable in Israel?" Samuel said, "Is it not for thee and for all thy father's house?" In order that he might fit himself for his high office, God gave Saul another heart and turned him into another man. But Saul was not faithful to his place or to the God who had put him there. In spite of the tears and prayers of Samuel, in spite of the repeated warnings which came to him, Saul went at length to his own place. That was the burden of David's eloquent dirge and lament over Saul; the fact that he had come to a miserable end, slain and desecrated and mutilated by his foes, his bow and sword vilely cast away, "as though he had not been anointed with oil."

Ah, had we the eloquence of David, what dirges we could sing over those who fell away from the place which God intended for them and went instead to their own place. How often, could we know the history that lies hidden back of those faces which pass us on the street, they would speak to us in tones of sadness and warning of high places to which they had been called, but from which they have fallen away, perhaps despairing now of ever occupying the place they might have occupied and which God had chosen for them. One of the most moving things and most powerful things in all the writings of Charles Dickens is that passage in the *Tale of Two Cities* where he describes Sydney Carton ascending the stairs to his dismal lodgings and throwing himself with a flood of tears on his wretched bed as he thinks of what he might have done with his talents and the place he might have occupied, had he not cast it all away by the folly of his dissipation.

II. We Choose Our Own Place in This World

Peter was referring, of course, to the final place and destiny of Judas, when he said, "He went to his own place." But that final place was linked to, and was the result of, the place which Judas chose for himself here in this life. Not only, then, do we choose our final place and destiny, but we choose our own place in this world. Hour by hour, day by day, month by month, year by year, by every thought, desire, imagination, and act we choose a place for ourselves here and build for ourselves the house of the soul.

Imagine, if you will, two men as they go forth tomorrow morning to live the life of that one day. This man commences it without a prayer. Perhaps he ushers in the day with ugliness of temper and churlishness of behavior toward his wife or his family. When he goes to his work and place of business, he provokes others to wrath and resentment. When he speaks of others he does so with envy or malice. Thus pass the hours of the day, and when the man comes back to his home from which he started out in the morning, he comes a dreaded, rather than a welcome, visitor. That man has his place, and it is no uncertain place. Did he have all the gold of Croesus, his place is to be shunned by all who desire happiness and peace of mind. No one forced that place on him; he chose it and fashioned it from the earliest hour of the day until the last. The life that he has lived this day is now his companion for the night and a part of his nature for the morrow; and if, in addition to his harsh and unfriendly conduct there has been dishonesty or sinful indulgence, the man is not only robbed of the happiness and content that might have been his, but has for his companion that unpleasant visitor and that unceasing speaker, remorse. It is sad to see a man in such a place; but sadder still when one reflects that this is his own place, the very place that he has chosen.

How different from that man's place is the place of the man who greets the day with prayer and thanks unto God, and goes forth to his work assisting and encouraging others as he has opportunity, provoking not to wrath, but to good works; if meeting evil, returning good for evil, and forbearing in love; the man who hopeth all things, believeth all things, thinketh no evil, rejoiceth not in iniquity, but rejoiceth in the truth; who suffers long and is kind. Night may find him weary, but content, for he is near to the fountain of love; and could we but see them, the angels of God wait upon him. If there is any sadness or heaviness in his heart, it is not because he thinks of those to whom he has been unjust or unkind, but because he grieves over the waywardness and sorrows and sins of others. He has chosen the more excellent way. He goes at the close of every day to his own place. We sometimes say that we are trying to "place" a man, to get the true conception of his personality and his character. Not always do we succeed in so doing, but always we do place ourselves. A man once said to me, a man who had fallen into great trouble and deep waters, "I was the architect of my own misfortune."

III. The Future Place

Judas went to his own place in the world to come. We would like to think of it as a place of happiness and worship; a place where the qualities of goodness and mercy, of love to God and charity to man which here survived the cold winter of this life, blossom and flower in all their beauty and fragrance; a place where memories of the days that were past sing their songs to cheer and gladden the heart; a place where the man who had lived upon the earth in a society where the good and evil mingled as the wheat and the tares, now has for his associates and companions only those who love the Lord and whose hearts are inclined to virtue. But, alas, when we put Judas in such a place we feel a strange incongruity in such an association. Judas in that place would be out of place. No; it was a different kind of place that Judas had chosen. Wise, chastened, and restrained, Peter makes no effort to lift the veil that covers the place of Judas, and all others who go out from the presence of the Lord. All that he says is, "He went to his own place."

We deal with a great mystery when we speak about the life to come, and there is some truth in what Dr. Brown in his *Religio Medici* says about our ignorance of that life, when he likens our conversation concerning it to the conversation of two unborn babes in the womb about the life of this world. Yet there are great principles which, upon the authority of Scriptures, we can lay down about that life to come. There is no reason to think that death, which solves so many problems and answers so many questions, makes any change in the moral character of the soul. Certainly the moral laws go on working there just as here. "He which is filthy, let him be filthy still: and he that is righteous, let him be righteous still." "As the tree falleth, so let it lie." There will be, no doubt, an infinite development of good for those who have chosen the good in this life, and likewise a development of evil, without the restraints and without the mitigations to the stings of remorse which obtain in this life.

The fact of the future life, and especially the fact of retribution in the future life, is a sadly neglected truth today. There are four great convictions—that there is a God; that there is a soul; that there is a life to come; and that there is judgment to come. You cannot dismiss retribution without dismissing God. It is not so much a truth that is brought to us from the outside, although revelation confirms it, but a deep instinct, a deep yearning, sometimes a deep dread, within the spirit of man. Yet it is a heavy subject, and the fate of the finally impenitent is one that we contemplate with awe, sometimes with deep questionings. For all who may be troubled on that subject, there is relief in these words of Peter about Judas; "He went to his own place," the place he had asked for and chosen in this life.

"Still, as of old, man by himself is priced;
For thirty pieces Judas sold himself, not Christ."

Peter does not say that God sent Judas to that place, but that he went to it himself. Future retribution is not a capricious assignment of punishment; not so much what is done to a man by the great Judge, but what a man does to himself. "I myself am heaven and hell."

Judas went to his own place in spite of Christ, not because of Christ. All that Jesus said to the other disciples, save what he said after Judas had gone out into the night, he said to Judas also. Judas did not go unwarned to his doom. I like to think that the washing of his feet at the Supper by Jesus and the words of Jesus, "What thou doest, do quickly," and again, when he called him "Friend" in the Garden of Gethsemane, were last appeals to Judas to turn before it was too late. But Judas would not turn. I have no doubt that one of the chief elements of future punishment will be the consciousness a man has that what he now endures and suffers he chose for himself.

This is a solemn subject; but let us think, in closing, of another place, the place to which God calls us, the place for which every soul is fitted by reason of its creation in the image of God. "I go," said Christ, "to prepare a place for you." That is true, not only of the life to come, but of this present life. You can lose a place or an opportunity in this world, and it is gone forever. Someone else fills it; but God keeps your empty place waiting for you. As Jonathan said to David, "Thou shalt be missed, for thy place shall be empty." Recently, there was the story of a mother whose wayward son had gone out from her home. For years the mother had been waiting for him to return, and always at night there was a light burning in the window, and always in her heart, too, was burning the hope that her son would come home. The other day she died, and before her son came home. Now the light has gone out in the window. But, thanks be to God, the light in the window of our Father's house never goes out! Whenever the soul turns back to God, God sees us afar off, as in Christ's matchless tale, the father saw the returning and penitent son afar off, "and ran, and fell on his neck, and kissed him."

AMNON

III

"Amnon had a friend"

II Samuel 13: 3

TONIGHT we have one of the most popular epitaphs. In some of the old cemeteries, "At rest," or, "May he rest in peace," occurs frequently on the headstones. The epitaph of this evening, "Amnon had a friend," is one which occurs very often. Substitute for Amnon some other name, and remember that we are speaking of cemeteries where not bodies but souls lie buried, and you will understand what I mean when I say that "Amnon had a friend" is a popular epitaph.

Amnon had a friend! But for that friend, he might have been kept back from committing a fearful sin. He had conceived a desire which he knew to be dangerous, lawless, and wicked. Between him and the commission of that sin there intervened every obstacle and every consideration which God can place between a man and his sin. There was the warning and the restraining voice of conscience, not yet grieved into silence. There was the gentle appeal of frailty and innocence. There was the dread of a father's anger and a brother's revenge, and the fear of the judgment of God. Yet, in spite of all these obstacles, Amnon succumbed to his temptation. The brutal deed was done, the law of God and the law of man were broken and trampled under his wicked feet.

Judgment did not tarry long. "Some men's sins are open beforehand, going before to judgment; and some men they follow after." The Apostle means there that in the case of some evildoers their judgment is long delayed, even until the next world. But in other cases the judgment follows quickly upon the heels of transgression. It was so in this case of Amnon. His heinous crime was quickly avenged. As he sat half-drunken at the shearing feast of his half-brother Absalom, the unpitying dagger of judgment was buried in his heart, and the sin-laden soul, with no opportunity to redress the wrong it had committed, and with no moment to seek either the forgiveness of man or of offended heaven, was hurried into eternity to stand before the Searcher of all hearts.

There was one other man who ought to have been killed at that shearing feast, and that man was Jonadab, the friend of Amnon. He was the friend who ruined Amnon. But for his aid and his arrangements, Amnon might have kept back from his enormity. Jonadab opened the way for Amnon. But when Amnon had reached the end of the road, and the dagger of retribution gleamed before his terrified eyes, the man who had helped him start on that path was not at hand to share in the punishment. He rarely is.

Amnon had a friend! That was his epitaph. It is the true epitaph of many a broken life. That brief sentence tells the story of many a man who has disappointed his own hopes and the prayers of those who loved him and dreamed for him. It tells the secret of the bitterness of many a sad and heavy hearted person who today goes mechanically about his work, his mind all the while turning with bitterness back to the ill-starred day when he met the friend who slew him. In many a life that once followed Jesus Christ and honored him as Saviour and King, but who now has no faith and no hope, or is following some of the gods made by the fancies and desires of men, that is the secret of the backsliding and apostasy—he had a friend.

I. The Power of the Social Principle

God divided man into men, said Seneca, that they might have friendship one for another. It is not good for man to be alone. All nature, from man down to the things that crawl in the dust or swim in the sea, bears witness to the social instinct which God hath planted in the whole creation. Where human friendships are denied him, man will make friends with the lower animals. Those who have become alienated or embittered from their fellow-men will yet witness to the great law of their nature by lavishing affection upon horses or dogs or birds. In the days when the Bastile was a living horror, a prisoner confined in the solitude of his cell made friends with a spider that he had found there and gave it the care and the affection of his mind and heart, until his brutal jailers discovered this insect amelioration of his lot and destroyed the spider.

Even in the Godhead we see the working of the social principle. Our God is not revealed to us in the Scriptures as a lonely solitary Being, forever dwelling by himself in thick and unapproachable darkness, but as a God of three Persons, the Father, the Son, the Holy Spirit. Unitarianism may be the logic of the human mind, but Trinitarianism is the theology of the heart, and out of the heart are the issues of life. All good things grow through the contact of mind with mind and heart with heart. Christianity started its campaigns of victory in the world by the fisherman Andrew bringing his brother Simon to Jesus. Jesus called about him twelve men as friends and companions, and of those twelve there were three sets of brothers, James and John, Peter and Andrew, and (probably) John the Less and the other Judas. True Christians do not get out a Bible and a hymn book on the Lord's Day and worship God by themselves, but they seek out the church where they that love the Lord can speak with one another in psalms and hymns and spiritual songs. The social principle is the chief factor through which both good and evil work out their issues of life and death.

II. The Baneful Influence of Wrong Friendships

Like the greatest and the best of God's gifts, this gift of companionship and friendship can be perverted and abused. When that takes place its power for evil is as great as its power for good. Theologians have discussed the question as to whether or not sin could exist in complete isolation. If there were just one man in the world, could that man be a sinner? The influence of this question has been carried over into the next life by those who believe that men who died godless and impenitent in this world may repent and be restored in the next life. One of the conditions which they think conducive to repentance and reformation is the complete isolation and loneliness of the soul. Shut off from every other soul, the man will lose all love for sin and hunger and thirst after righteousness, and seeking God, even in the solitude of his place of punishment, will not fail of finding him.

That is interesting as a theory of theology. But confining our thought to this life, and what we know and see on this side of the grave, we observe that evil is done, spread, perpetuated by the social principle. There may be, there is Original Sin, but there are no original sinners. We have our own incitements to evil within our breasts. But if there were no evil persons in our world about us, and if there were no tempters, would there be any transgression? What I mean is that men do not suddenly blossom out by themselves into sinners. They must first breathe the tainted atmosphere that has been poisoned by other men, and thus evil makes its way to their hearts. From the thief and the drunkard to the man who mocks at God, the wrongdoer had to get the suggestion from another man. The story of Eden, wonderful in its fidelity to the facts of human experience, squares with human nature in this particular of temptation. The incitement to question the command of God, and then to break the commandment, came from a tempter without, who told them that they could eat and not die. Just as physical disease persists and spreads from generation to generation by man touching man, so is it with the spread and contagion of moral evil.

III. How Men Are Wrecked Through Their Friendships

Were I asked to name the chief peril of the great city for the young men and the young women who every year pour into it, seeking their careers, I should say, without any hesitation, it is the peril of hastily formed and ill-chosen friendships and intimacies. We are to be held strictly accountable for the character, the kind of life, that in the end we render up to God, in the day when he shall try the hearts of all men. Yet that character depends to a great extent upon the conduct of other men and the influence of their conduct upon us. That law we are always recognizing. Two men were discussing the welfare of a young man in whom they were both interested, seeking to save him from moral ruin. One said to the other, "Do you think him beyond further effort?" "I am afraid," said the other, "there is, humanly speaking, no hope. He has taken with company that forbids it."

In the casting of the lots of life, it would appear that men of equal parts are seldom thrown together. Instead of seeing a bad man, or evilly inclined man, with a weak will, in company with a good man with a strong will, and unable to resist the influence of the good, what we more frequently see is a bad man with a strong will in company with a good man with a weak will, who feels the imprint and pressure of that stronger nature and soon follows him in the path of evil. That is the drama that is being acted out day after day, year after year in the midst of our great cities. Men are enticed, and being enticed, they yield. A young man confided in me recently how he had fallen before temptation, and how even in the company of his evil companions his better nature was condemning him, and how he thought particularly how his conduct would shock and grieve his mother. Yet he consented. He went with his friends. He had a friend.

The method of persuasion employed by Jonadab upon this occasion is still a very popular and effective one. He said to the hesitating Amnon, "Art thou not a king's son?" If so, get what you want, do as you please. If one appeals, or seems to appeal, to conscience, to the principles of religious training, to the memory of those who love and trust him, at once the subtle tempter whispers tauntingly in his ear: "Art thou not a king's son? Are you going to be frightened by Sunday school lessons and prayers learned at your mother's knee? Be a man, and get what you want!" Alas! alas! for the slain souls who have gone down deep into destruction because they were taunted by temptation in an assertion of this false independence, which is the independence of the fool.

Wherever a soul perishes, somewhere there lurks a tempter, a Jonadab. In this audience tonight there will be not a few men who will recall with a sense of pain and shame and humiliation the names of certain persons who were their friends, and through whose friendship they were carried along into some sinful course, to blot out the memory of which they would willingly cut off their right hand. But if you did go through unscathed, if you were of stronger will and said to the tempter, "Get thee behind me," still can you not—I know that you can, and that you will —recall at least one or two friends whose friendship, now looking back, you can see was dangerous in the extreme? Your soul was in peril. Your life was at stake. You devoutly thank God that he led you out unhurt.

Try your friendships. Test your friends. Be sure that no man who is not a good man can be a good friend. If he lack that fundamental virtue, his gifts of personality and learning will make him all the more dangerous. I would that I could meet every train coming into the city bringing its precious cargo of young lives starting out on the great adventure of the world; that I could encounter every young man as he comes to the doors of college and school; that I could meet them as they throng to shop and factory and office, and as they come back to their rooming houses, and say to them all, "Who is your friend?" Your home training may have been good; your present work exacting; the draw of your hope and ambitions strong and upward; but let me warn you that there is a power which can, for good or for evil, relegate all these to a secondary place, and that is the power of your friendships. Character declares itself quickly and just as driving through the country on a spring day you can tell what kind of trees and flowers you are passing without turning to look with your eyes, because you catch their fragrance, so is it in the matter of friendship. The wholesome and the unwholesome, the fragrant and the tainted, quickly declare themselves to him who seeks for the best and who fears, as one ought to fear, the worst.

IV. Safeguards in Friendships

1. *Fixed principles.* It is the man who has not decisively made up his mind as to right and wrong who is influenced for evil by his companionship. Thomas Arnold of Rugby, speaking of this, once said: "Of all the painful things connected with my employment nothing is equivalent to the grief of seeing a boy come to the school innocent and promising, and tracing the corruption of his character from the influence of the temptations around him, in the very place which ought to have strengthened it and improved it. But in most cases those who come with a character of positive good are benefited; it is the neutral and indecisive characters which are apt to be decided for evil by schools, as they would, in fact, by any other temptation."

When a man is not traveling himself in any particular direction, it is a simple matter for one going in the wrong direction to persuade him to go with him. Instead of being influenced by others, have such strong purposes of right in your heart and such antipathy for evil that you will be the magnet to influence others.

2. *The courage of loneliness and isolation.* The right kind of man can find the right kind of friends if he wills to do it. But even if that were impossible, even if one had to choose between having no friends at all, or friends who are no help to one, there should not be a moment's hesitation. Choose solitude and right and the interrogation of a good conscience rather than the happy evening with friends who make you compromise your principles, who take the edge off your good resolutions and becloud your faith and leave a bad taste in your soul. The great and successful men have been those who owed their power, not more to their ascendance over others than to the fact that they themselves permitted others to have no evil influence over them. In any walk of life, especially in this highest of all enterprises, the acquisition of moral character, one of the chief secrets of success lies in the ability to make ourselves inaccessible to the wrong influence of others.

What we need is a noble independence and a rigid adherence to our own standards of right. Well for every young man if he had the courage of Wesley at Christ College, when he determined to have no men for intimate friends who would not help him on the way to heaven. If every young man and every young woman here tonight made that their rule, there would be many quenched intimacies and many broken friendships. The more I see of it, the more I believe that the men who rise high, who come through the furnace of the world unscathed, are the men who have had the strength of character to come out and be separate from those whose influence was not for their good. They had the courage of loneliness.

One of the most successful preachers of Scotland, Ambrose Shepherd, writes thus of his youth: "I have already alluded to my experience in a hard school. Indulge me if I return to it for a moment. My earlier years were spent in a Lancashire cloth mill. In it I wrought from morning to night side by side with youths of my own age and men who were older. For the most part, young and old, they were practiced in almost every conceivable coarse and brutal way of casting their existence as rubbish to the void. But I think I can truthfully say that, while I tried to be loyal to the conditions of contract, and as a comrade in the ranks was not unpopular, yet they knew that neither within those grim walls nor without them was I of their world."

Have your own world! Have the courage to stay in that world and breathe its pure air, though you may be lonely.

Chief of all the safeguards in friendship is the friendship of Christ. Here is the Friend who loves you with the deepest love, for greater love hath no man than this, that a man lay down his life for his friend. Here is the Friend who will do you good and not evil all the days of your life. Here is the

Friend who can do what even the most faithful and best loved friend could never do—he can take away the stain and soil of your sin. He is the Friend that sticketh closer than a brother. Do you know that Friend?

THE MAN WHO WON AND THEN LOST

IV

"Alas, my brother!"

I Kings 13: 30

ON the main road leading from Bethel down to Judah, a strange sight. On one side of the road, a fierce lion; on the other side, an ass, saddled and grazing, unafraid; on the road between the lion and the ass, the body of a prophet, mauled and mangled by the lion. A strange and unusual roadside spectacle. When the prophet's mangled body was buried, this was the epitaph put on his grave, "Alas, my brother!"

Jeroboam, the son of Nebat, who made Israel to sin, cared nothing for the true religion. Nevertheless, he looked upon it as a useful superstition in holding together the revolted Kingdom of Israel. He feared that when the people went up to Jerusalem to worship, the old memories of Jerusalem and the temple would begin to move upon them and make them regret that they had broken with the Kingdom of Judah. To guard against this, he invented a hybrid worship of his own, making two golden calves and setting them up as gods, one at Dan and the other at Bethel. Not content with making priests out of the lowest of the people, Jeroboam himself played the priest.

He was thus blasphemously engaged in offering incense at the golden calf at Bethel, when a nameless man of God, who, like Elijah, emerging suddenly, like a specter out of the mists, stood before Jeroboam and cried against the altar, saying, "O altar, altar!" In times of religious declension and apostasy, God puts great responsibility and honor upon courageous, indomitable, and incorruptible messengers who will speak without fear of favor his truth. This man of God was such a messenger. In his denunciation of this calf worship, he offered a remarkable prediction, saying that in the future a king of Judah, Josiah, would offer the priests of idol worship upon this altar, and that men's bones should be burnt upon it. Three hundred and sixty years later, this prophecy was remarkably fulfilled by the great king and reformer, Josiah. One of the first acts of his reign was to break down the altar of Bethel and stamp it to powder and burn the grove about it.

As Josiah was engaged in his labor of judgment and destruction, he saw graves in the vicinity, and learning that they were the sepulchers of priests who had ministered at this altar, he had their bones taken out of the graves and burned them upon the altar, just as this nameless prophet had predicted. In the Old Testament we have several classes of predictions and prophecies. First, those which refer to the future of Israel, and many of which are fulfilled. Second, those which predict the coming of Christ, and which have been fulfilled; and third, those which foretell the overthrow of contemporary heathen kingdoms, such as Egypt, Babylon, Assyria, and Tyre. The ruins of those once world empires are today a mighty witness to the truth of the Old Testament. But in addition to these predictions of great world events, or personalities, there are those which deal with individuals or particular events and happenings, and to this class belongs the prediction concerning Jeroboam's altar, remarkably fulfilled three and a half centuries afterward. To predict that a thing will come to pass, and then bring it to pass centuries later, this, or nothing, is the power of God.

As a sign of the fulfilment of this prophecy, the man of God told Jeroboam that the altar would be rent and the ashes poured upon the ground. The enraged king stretched out his hand to smite the man of God, and was immediately smitten himself, for his hand dropped by his side, withered and paralyzed. The king's wrath then changed to entreaty and he begged the prophet to pray for him that his hand might be restored. This the man of God did, and the arm was healed. Having failed by violence, Jeroboam now tries flattery and bribery. He had seduced to his cause, and from the worship of God, many another prophet, and he felt confident that he could handle this one. So he invited the man of God to come home with him and refresh himself, and told him that he would give him a reward. But the man of God refused to go, telling the king that when he set out on this errand the Word of the Lord had charged him that he was not to go into any man's house to eat bread or drink water, and that he was not to return by the way he had come. These instructions, no doubt, were to insure the faithful fulfilment of his commission, and also to show God's abhorrence of what had transpired at Bethel. True to his commission, the man of God set out on his return journey, taking a different route from that by which he had come.

In Bethel there dwelt an old prophet, evidently more aged than venerable. He was a strange mixture of good and evil. He was one of those prophets who had acquiesced in Jeroboam's bastard worship, and yet he had not altogether forgotten the worship of God. He was a strange mixture of wavering inspiration and desire for good, together with ignoble cowardice and apostasy. But the old man was stirred within himself when his sons came home and told him what had transpired at the altar. The story of the man of God's heroic conduct evidently awakened some lingering desire in this apostate prophet to associate himself again with a true messenger of God. Perhaps he thought that in this way his lost prestige could be established. Or he may have fancied that by getting the man of God to return and break bread with him he would curry favor with the king, whose invitation had been scorned. At all events, whatever his motives, he sadled his ass and set out in pursuit of the man of God. At length he came upon him resting by the roadside under the shade of an oak. When he learned that he was the man of God, he invited him to go home with him and eat bread and drink water. The man of God refused and said to the old prophet what he had said to Jeroboam. With a ready lie on his lips, the prophet asserted that he, too, was a prophet and that he had received a revelation from the Lord, telling him to go after the man of God and bring him back to his house. Taken in with this clever lie, the man of God returned to Bethel and entered into the house of the old prophet. As they sat eating and drinking together, the old prophet received this time a genuine revelation, and pronounced the judgment of God upon the man of God whom he had thus seduced, telling him that because of his disobedience he would not come unto the sepulcher of his fathers. It must have been with a heavy heart, with deep regret over his blunder and disobedience, and with the heavy and oppressive dread of impending judgment that the man of God got on his beast and the second time started for Judah. Some hours afterward, wayfaring men coming into Bethel reported that they had seen a strange sight by the roadside. On one side, a fierce lion; on the other side, a saddled ass grazing; and between them the dead body of a prophet. The old prophet knew immediately who the man was, and rode off to the place where the body lay. He took up the body and carried it back to the city and buried it in his own grave. Filled with remorse at the part he had played in the downfall of the man of God, he requested of his sons that when he was dead they should bury him by the side of the man of God, and standing over his grave he lamented and mourned over him, saying, "Alas, my brother!"

"Alas, my brother!" This is a true epitaph, for when we come to the end of this strange, and yet thought-provoking story, and see the fate of one who did so nobly, and yet fell and failed at the last, our feeling is one of sorrow. "Alas, my brother!"

If we had been handing out judgment on this occasion, it would have been the old seducing prophet upon whom our punishment would have fallen, for it seems to us that of the two he is the guilty one, and that the lion slew the wrong man. But God's ways are not our ways, nor his thoughts our thoughts. The fall and judgment of this man of God is a powerful and dramatic illustration of the truth that he that endureth to the end shall be saved, and that not one of God's commandments can be broken with impunity.

There is nothing so patient and persistent as temptation. The man of God, when first called to perform this dangerous mission to cry against the altar of Jeroboam, resisted the temptation to draw back because of fear for his personal safety. He also resisted the temptation of flattery by Jeroboam to be a guest to his house. The bribe, too, which Jeroboam offered him he put behind him. Then, when the prophet first invited him to return, he resisted that temptation, also, only to go down before a final temptation. The way Satan kept on the trail of his man of God is a picture of the grim persistency and tireless patience of temptation. When the devil had been thrice repulsed by Jesus in the wilderness, he left him; but, the evangelist significantly adds, "for a season." Temptation leaves us for a season, and then comes back at unexpected times and in unexpected manner.

Men resist and conquer what seems to be the stronger temptation, only to go down before the less. When we see the man of God taking his rest under the oak tree by the roadside, we are sure that his dangerous mission has been successfully fulfilled, that he has resisted all temptations, and we feel like congratulating him upon his splendid conduct. Jeroboam's flattery, the offer of a bribe, the old prophet's invitation to go to his house, all that he has set aside.

He is a splendid picture as we see him riding out of Bethel on his beast, with his gray hair streaming in the wind, and we feel like calling to him, "Well done, thou good and faithful servant. None ever did better than thou hast done." But now, what bribes, threats, violence, and flattery could not effect is accomplished by the lie of an old broken-down and apostate prophet. Just when we think that this man has won a great victory we see him fall and go to his doom.

I read sometime after the war of a man who had fought through all the fearful engagements in Flanders with the Canadian army, and without a scar, only to meet his death by falling from a hay wagon when he came home. This is a picture of what often happens in the moral life of men. The man who stands firm in some great difficulty in the world goes down in a domestic skirmish. The man who overcomes a tiger appetite for strong drink yields to avarice. He who resists the hot and fearful whisper of lust goes down before bad temper and anger. He who bears the cross of some great trial like a martyr succumbs to the pin prick of some petty irritation or insult. David on several occasions, with magnificent self-control, refused to harm his great foe, King Saul, when he had him in his power. But the same David, immediately after this fine exhibition of magnanimous self-control, sets out on an errand of vengeance upon Nabal, who had refused him hospitality, a vengeance which would have left a whole town weltering in its blood, but for the timely intercession of the beautiful Abigail. There is something about a great temptation which arouses the resisting energies of the soul, and thus itself provides a sort of safeguard. The great temptation here, we think, was that of the powerful king of Israel, Jeroboam, and not that of this good-for-nothing old scoundrel, the apostate prophet. Yet it was the latter temptation which brought the prophet to his doom.

The man of God was deceived by an alleged revelation in the mouth of this lying prophet. But he ought to have known that God is not a man that he should lie, nor a son of man that he should repent. Moral standards do not change, and the safe and wise thing is to obey the first reactions of conscience. Go through the ranks of those who have been overcome of evil, and say to each one of them, "Did you feel this thing to be wrong when you were first tempted to do it? or was it only when you had gone far in the wrong course and had realized that the way of the transgressor is hard, that you felt the thing to be wrong?" What will his answer be? He will tell you that he knew it was wrong at the very beginning, that a voice spake clearly and unmistakably, and that his one regret is that he did not follow and obey that voice when he first heard it speak.

Since man is made in the image of God, and created so that he can do the will of God, moral failure is always sad. But the greatest sadness is when a good man, like this man of God, goes down before temptation. His fate shows that no one can count on his past record, and that every day he must watch and pray and fight. At noon, this man of God has a grand record. We are ready to put him in a niche of fame by the side of Moses, Samuel, and Elijah. But ere the sun sets, we see his dead body between the lion and the ass, and our farewell to him is, "Alas, my brother!" What counts is the end. You may overcome nine temptations, but if you go down before the tenth, the fall is no less real and no less disastrous. In the old Grecian myth, Orpheus with his lyre went through the infernal regions in quest of his lost wife, Eurydice. As he passed, Tantalus ceased for a moment from stooping to quench his thirst; Ixion's wheel stood still; the vulture ceased to tear the giant's liver; the daughters of Danaus rested from their futile toil, and Sisyphus sat on the rock to listen, and even the cheeks of the Furies were wet with tears, so compelling was the music of Orpheus, mourning for his lost companion. Pluto consented that he should take his wife with him to the upper air, but upon one condition, that he would not look on her until they reached the regions above. And hell held its breath as they passed on their way to the light. One by one the dreadful perils were passed. But just as they were on the verge of the upper world, Orpheus looked back, and all his labors were in vain. Eurydice had vanished. So it was with this man of God. Almost to the very close of the chapter he is magnificent in his courage, steadfastness, and faithfulness to the word of God. But at the last he looked back and was lost.

> "The gray-haired saint may fall at last,
> The surest guide a wanderer prove.
> Death only binds us fast
> To that bright shore of love."

He that endureth to the end shall be saved.

ABSALOM

V

"O Absalom, my son, my son!"

II Samuel 18: 33

HERE we have the saddest and the most beautiful epitaph in the Bible, the cry of David when he heard of the death of his son Absalom.

"Would it had been my own funeral!" I heard these words uttered once in the presence of death, and by the side of the dead. It was not a cry wrung from a soul that was in the paroxysm of its grief, and representing therefore only the emotion of a moment. Instead of that, it was a calm and measured wish. Hearing the words, time ran back for me twenty-nine centuries, and I stood by the gate of ancient Mahanaim, as David groped his way up the stone stairs to the chamber over the gate; and as he went I heard him cry, "O my son Absalom, my son, my son Absalom! would God I had died for thee, O Absalom, my son, my son!" It was that same ancient cry that I heard on this more recent day when I stood by the side of the broken in heart.

I. The Cry of Deep Grief and Sorrow

Here multitudes of those who sorrow have tuned their hearts to David's lamentation. That is the first thing I read in this saddest and yet most beautiful epitaph. In the pain of his heart David wishes that life for him were over; that it was he who lay dead in the tangled forest of Ephraim, rather than the golden-haired Absalom. Probably everyone, before he finishes his journey and accomplishes his appointed probation in this life of trial, has some moment in which he might wish that he were dead. The bright noonday sky of life has suddenly become clouded and dark, and it does not seem possible that the sun will ever shine again. Here, then, we have the sigh of a soul for peace and for rest, a peace and a rest which it feels can be secured only by ceasing to live. That was what that mourning friend meant when he said, "Would it had been my own funeral!" "Would God I had died for thee!" It is a cry as old as Job. "Why died I not from the womb? . . . . For now I should have lain still and been quiet; I should have slept; then had I been at rest. . . . . There the wicked cease from troubling; and there the weary be at rest." It is a cry as old as the Psalmist, when fearfulness and trembling came upon him. "O that I had wings like a dove! for then would I flee away, and be at rest. Lo, then would I wander far off, and remain in the wilderness. I would hasten my escape from the stormy wind and tempest." It is a cry as old as Elijah, pursued by the wicked Jezebel, and convinced that his witness for God to an adulterous generation had been in vain. "It is enough; now, O Lord, take away my life; for I am not better than my fathers." An old cry, and yet ever new, as new as that mother who but yesterday saw her babe fade like a flower, blasted by a winter wind; as old as royal David's cry in the chamber over the gate, when the runner brought him word that loved Absalom was dead in the thicket of the wilderness. As new as that one who but yesterday saw himself parted from the companion of fifty years of pilgrimaging through this life, and was left to be brave alone; as new as that prisoner of hope who today heard the gates of opportunity close against him forever with harsh and heartless echo; as new as that trusting and confiding heart whose love could think no evil and only believe all things and hope all things good, but now in the bitterness of soul discovers that its love and trust and confidence have been rewarded with scorn and infidelity.

In his enthusiastic support of the long wars with France, Edmund Burke seemed never to think of the sorrows those wars brought home to multitudes of hearts. But when his own son was killed in battle, it was as if all world politics and personal pursuits had lost their meaning. "The storms," he writes, "have gone over me, and I lie like one of those old oaks which the late hurricane has scattered about me. I am stripped of all my honors; I am torn up by the roots and lie prostrate on the earth. I am alone. I have none to meet my enemies in the gate. I live in an inverted order. They who ought to have succeeded me have gone before me. They who should have been to me as posterity are in the place of ancestors." Charles Sumner, great Senator from Massachusetts and eloquent pleader for the slaves and for the Union, drank a bitter cup of sorrow and disappointment in his domestic life. When he was struck with death, there lay on his table a volume of Shakespeare, this passage in *Henry VIII*, probably the last lines upon which his eyes ever gazed, marked with his own hand:

> "Would I were dead! If God's good will were so;
> For what is in this world but care and woe?"

This, then, is the first note that I hear in this cry of David over the death of his son. In reality, it is a cry not for death, but for life more abundant. It is a witness within the sacred place of man's life, like the virgin's lamp burning ever in the holy shrine, and which speaks of perfect and sinless life for which the soul was formed.

II. The Cry of Retribution

Knowing as we do the circumstances of Absalom's death, and the history of his life and the history of

David's life, it is impossible to escape the conclusion that a very real part of David's cup of bitterness and grief was in the consciousness that God was visiting upon him his own sins. It was not only Absalom who had been judged, but David. So God visits the iniquities of the fathers upon the children unto the third and fourth generation. David, no doubt, reflected that had his own life been free from the great transgression, Absalom might have come to a different end. As he groped his way up those stairs to the chamber over the gate, he must have seen the beautiful face of Bathsheba, the face of murdered Uriah, and the face of Nathan, the prophet of the Lord, who said to him, "Thou art the man," and who told him that, although his sin had been forgiven, the natural and temporal penalties of it would afflict him all through this life, that the sword would never depart from his house. Yes, that must have been what David was thinking of, and the consciousness of his own sin makes him utter his beautiful, pathetic, but impossible cry, that he himself had had the darts of Joab driven through his breast and not Absalom. Retribution creates a solemn and awful music, and it is that music which we hear in David's broken-hearted cry, "Would God I had died for thee, O Absalom, my son, my son!"

III. The Cry of Grief Over a Wasted Life

Absalom was a gifted man. From the very beginning of his life, he had the deep love of his father,

David, who called him Absalom, "the father, or the source, of peace." But what a sad misnomer the name was! He had attractive qualities which won the allegiance and love of powerful men in his kingdom, and the common people whose hearts he stole heard him gladly and followed him in his great rebellion. He ought to have counted for something great and good in the world, but that was the end he came to. Buried like a dead dog in a pit in the forest, and a pile of stones heaped over him.

Absalom had reared for himself a costly pillar or mausoleum in the king's dale. That was the tomb which he expected to occupy. There his flawless body, arrayed in royal robes and prepared for the sepulcher, was to be laid away with a kingdom's lamentation. Succeeding generations would tarry by that tomb and exclaim, "Here lies Absalom, the son of David."

How different was the grave into which he was cast like a dead dog. Instead of resting in the marble mausoleum, that flawless body, once without a blemish, from the sole of his foot to the crown of his head, lay gashed and broken at the bottom of the forest pit, covered with a heap of stones, and with none save his broken-hearted father to mourn over him. But yonder in the king's dale stands his pillar. The rising sun gilded with glory its finely cut stone, its silver and its gold; the noonday sun halted to behold its beauty, and night draped its white shaft with her ethereal robe. But it was a tomb without an occupant, a pillar without a prince, a monument without a man.

The stone pile and the pillar. Absalom is not the only man who planned for a pillar and ended beneath a stone pile. There are multitudes who have hopes and ambitions as high as Absalom, but who, because of a lack of reverence and purity and faith in God, will have for their grave, as it were, instead of a pillar a stone pile, and over them their broken hopes, their blighted ambitions, their perished opportunities—all that some broken-hearted father, mother, sister, can say is, what in the depth of his grief and disappointment David said over Absalom, "Would God I had died for thee."

David's prayer was as vain and impossible as it was sad and beautiful. It was not possible that David could take the place of Absalom. No man can become the substitute for another before the broken law of God. None may take another's guilt, or bear another's punishment, or drink another's cup of woe. But to this there is one grand exception, and that is the Cross whereon Christ died for sinners. No matter what the blunders, mistakes, wasted opportunities of life, no matter what the sentence of guilt and retribution, there is One, and only One, who is permitted to take your place. Christ can and will die for you. He will drink the cup of your sin and woe. It is his glory and his power to take our place on the Cross. The sad and pathetic epitaphs of this world spoken over broken and failed lives, "Would God I had died for thee," by the infinite power and mercy of God and Christ are changed into that grand declaration of hope, and let it ring out now to every prodigal, to every wanderer, to all who may feel that they have sinned and failed, "I have died for thee. I have redeemed thee with an Everlasting Love."

JEROBOAM

VI

"Jeroboam, the son of Nebat, who made Israel to sin"

I Kings 22: 52

THE burial ground of the Old Testament is one of the most interesting in the world. Here are the tombs of kings, prophets, princes, peasants, patriarchs, judges, good men and bad men. Striking and quaint are the epitaphs that meet our eye as we wander through this cemetery. Here is one of them, and lest it should be forgotten, it is repeated, in substance, more than twenty times, "Jeroboam, the son of Nebat, who made Israel to sin."

The sunset of the reign of Solomon is in striking contrast with the early part of his life. It is hard to believe that this Solomon, sunken in sensuality, and surrounded with idols and with strange women, is the same Solomon who knelt on Gibeon's slopes and asked God for wisdom rather than riches, and for virtue rather than fame, the same Solomon who built the Temple and dedicated it with his beautiful prayer. God told him that the kingdom would be rent from him; but—and how touching and beautiful is the allusion—God says he will not do it in the days of Solomon, "for David thy father's sake." But when Solomon was dead, and Rehoboam his son was king, God raised adversaries against him. Rehoboam received wise counsel from the old and experienced men of the kingdom; but instead of taking their advice, he followed the Youth Movement of his day and foolishly oppressed his people. Among the protestants and patriots was Jeroboam.

Jeroboam, the son of Nebat, was a young man of great industry, zeal, and capacity, who had been appointed by Solomon to take charge of the engineering work on the fortifications at Millo. When Solomon learned of the prophecy that the kingdom was to be given to Jeroboam, he sought to kill him; but Jeroboam escaped death by flight into Egypt. When Solomon was dead he returned to Israel and led the revolt against Rehoboam. A new kingdom, made up of the Ten Tribes, was now set up with Jeroboam as king. Jeroboam was afraid that if he permitted the people to go up to worship every year at the Temple they would be won back to the Kingdom of Judah. Therefore, he set up a mongrel religion of his own, administered by priests of his own choosing, whom he had raised up from the lowest of the people. At Dan and Bethel, the two extremities of the kingdom, he set up golden calves, and said to the people, "Behold, thy gods!" The result of this was that the people were led into idolatry. Centuries afterward, when Jeroboam had been long in his grave, what he had introduced into the kingdom continued to corrupt and lead astray the people of Israel. Hence, that monotonous refrain of the historical books of the Old Testament, sounding like a dirge, "Jeroboam, the son of Nebat, who made Israel to sin."

That is Jeroboam's epitaph—"He made Israel to sin." Let us stop by his grave and meditate on this epitaph. Temptation is a universal fact. Whereever man is, there is temptation. If you go down into one of the limestone caverns of Bermuda, you can hear flowing darkly away the waters of a subterranean river. Hearkening to the flowing of that stream, there may come to you the thought that while kingdoms have risen and fallen and generations have come and gone on the surface of the earth above you, that river has ever been flowing darkly through that cavern. So forever flows the river of temptation through human life. This is why a sermon on temptation is always timely. No one beats the air when one speaks on this subject. But generally when we speak of temptation we deal with it exclusively on the side of the one who is tempted. We think of the temptations to which we are subject, and through which we might be led to do that which is evil and betray our souls. But tonight we look at the other side of temptation, the side which is rarely mentioned, and that is, the part played by the tempter, or the sin of leading others into sin. Jeroboam's sin was in itself a very great one, as it related to the king himself; but what the Bible emphasizes about Jeroboam's sin is the effect that it had upon others.

Evil is latent in human nature. The seeds of original sin grow in every heart; but that latent and original evil is drawn out by the example and suggestion and invitation of others. That is the way sin started to do its work in the world. Before man fell the tempter came and spoke to him.

Sometimes the temptation is a wilful, deliberate, and truly diabolical effort to seduce another soul into evil. There is the fearful desire and purpose to bring others down and sully the white innocence of another soul. More frequently, perhaps, the temptation which leads others astray may be, for him who does the tempting, the unconscious influence for evil of what he says or what he does. But in the end one is just as hurtful and fatal as the other.

I. False Beliefs

There are those who tempt others into wrong belief, into false forms of worship. That was what Jeroboam did. His chief thought was to preserve the independence of his kingdom; but the means which he chose to accomplish that end led the people of Israel into idolatry. It was easier to go to Dan or Bethel than it was to go to Jerusalem, and, no doubt, the golden calves had their appeal for the people of Israel, just as the golden calf which Aaron made and which the people worshiped when Moses was in the mount. Either there is no true religion, or there are those speaking and teaching in the name of religion today who have a heavy responsibility upon them, an account which they must render to God, because they have led men and churches into forms of religion which are as remote from true Christianity as the calf worship at Dan and Bethel was from the true worship of Jehovah at Jerusalem.

Unbelief does not like to travel alone. It always seeks for a companion; it is a natural missionary. Would that friends of truth, and would that the true believers were as ready to speak for the faith that is in them as the worshipers of false gods are to testify to their false religion!

II. Sins of Desire, Pleasure, and Passion

These sins cannot be committed alone. They require others; and although with many the first thought is only that of gratification, with no purpose of injuring or contaminating others, that in the end is the result. Others are injured or corrupted that one may gratify his desire. The evil spirit in our Lord's parable was not content to dwell in his house by himself, but sought out seven other spirits, worse than himself.

"Woe to him," said the ancient prophet, Habakkuk, "that giveth his neighbor drink." This is a woe which they who tempt others to drink might well remember, and remembering it, tremble. A man told me recently of a scene he witnessed in one of the hotels of this city. At a table near where he was sitting was a young woman, a descendant of a man known everywhere for his godliness and high character. Her companion plied her with drink until she was so drunken that she had to be carried out of the dining-room.

I suppose that our Lord was speaking primarily of little children, for it was just after he had taken a little child and set him in their midst that the words were spoken, "Whoso shall offend one of these little ones which believe in me, it were better for him that a millstone were hanged about his neck, and that he were drowned in the depth of the sea." But what is true of leading astray a child is true of leading any soul astray. What a meeting that would be between two souls in the realm of the condemned, and one soul saying to the other, "I am here in the realm of the lost, forever shut out from hope and forgiveness and the face of God because of what you taught me to do, because of what you taught me to think." No, hell is not yet dispensed with; and one of the chief agents of its misery and retribution will undoubtedly be the consciousness that some souls will have that there are those who share that lost estate with them because they were tempted to evil through their invitation or example.

Think earnestly, then, about your example and your influence upon others. You are living in the midst of great and solemn realities. You are not a brick, or a stone, or a clod; neither is the one next to you. Human souls are the most sensitive things in the universe. Every thought that passes through your mind, every word and every deed, is like a hammer blow on the head of the chisel which touches another life. Take heed, therefore, to the outgoing of your life, to the echo of your voice, to the tread of your foot, to the touch of the finger of your influence.

There died recently at the age of eighty-five a man who was well known in London and throughout Great Britain as an apostle of temperance, partly because he gave up a fortune of $6,000,000 for conscience' sake and for the sake of his fellow-man.

Frederick N. Charrington was out one evening making a night of it with a group of friends. Strolling down one of London's most notorious streets, they passed a gin palace. Suddenly, a woman, ragged and pale, reeled out, her frail frame convulsed with sobs. She was clinging to a ruffian who was trying to shake her loose. "For God's sake," she cried, "give me a copper. I'm hungry, and the children are starving." But the man clenched his fist and struck her to the ground. Young Charrington and his friends rushed in to intervene and protect the woman. After the police had taken the couple away he happened to glance up at the illuminated sign over the saloon door, and there he read in letters of gold his own name—"Drink Charrington beer." "The message," afterward wrote this young man, "came to me then as it had come to the Apostle Paul. Here was the source of my family wealth. Then and there I raised my hands to heaven, that not another penny of that tainted money should come to me, and that henceforth I would devote my life to fighting the drink traffic." He had a sudden awakening to his responsibility and his influence, and saw that the earth was being cursed for his sake.

Woe to those who tempt others to sin. Woe, eternal woe! As Christ put it, millstone damnation! But blessing and eternal blessing to those who provoke others and tempt others to love and to good works, and who by their character and by their faith allure others heavenward.

GEHAZI

VII

"A leper as white as snow"

II Kings 5: 27

IN Westminster Abbey there is a part of the building known as the Poets' Corner, where many of England's great poets lie buried. Like Westminster, and other celebrated places of burial, the Bible Cemetery has its different sections and corners. There is the Prophets' Corner, the Apostles' Corner, the Judges' Corner, the Patriarchs' Corner, the Kings' Corner, and the Martyrs' Corner. But today we shall stop in the Liars' Corner. Here they lie buried, the notorious liars of the Bible. Here is Cain; and there are the eleven brothers of Joseph. Here is Achan, buried under a heap of stones, for his crime of stealing and lying. And over there lies Ananias, and close by his side his partner in avarice and lying, Sapphira. And here is a tomb with this strange epitaph on it—"*A leper as white as snow.*" Who is the man who is handed down to future ages as the complete and perfect leper —"a leper as white as snow"?

No man in the Bible is more sharply etched than the man with this epitaph on his tomb. He was a courteous and accomplished liar and hypocrite, and, like many of the most notorious liars, his lie was linked with the sin of avarice and covetousness. By poetic justice he was punished by being turned into a leper. His name is Gehazi. Gehazi ought to have had, might have had, a far different epitaph. There are those who struggle through adverse circumstances, beat down temptation, and in spite of an unfortunate environment win for themselves a noble epitaph. There are others who in spite of good example and inspiring associations and environment go down into their graves in disgrace with epitaphs of infamy upon their tomb. Such a man was Gehazi.

Gehazi and the Shunammite Woman

Gehazi was the friend and companion of one of the noblest and godliest men of the Bible, the "man of God," as he was called, Elisha. Gehazi had the unspeakable benefit and advantage of such an association. Yet in daily fellowship with one of the best and noblest men that ever came into the world, all that he did was to win for himself a leper's epitaph—"A leper as white as snow." The first time we hear of Gehazi is in connection with Elisha and the great woman of

Shunem. Whenever Elisha passed through Shunem on his errands of mercy or judgment he turned into this house to eat bread. This woman and her husband enjoyed Elisha's conversation and felt that his presence in their home was a benediction. One day she said to her husband: "I know that this Elisha is a holy man of God. Why not build an addition to our house, where we can have a special chamber for Elisha to stay in whenever he comes this way?" Her husband readily agreed to the proposal, and the chamber was built on the wall. It was furnished with a bed and a table and a stool and a candlestick. A good man does not need much for his comfort and maintenance in this world. This chamber that the man and woman at Shunem built for the entertainment of Elisha has given the name to the room where ministers are entertained, the "Prophet's Chamber."

One day, when Elisha lay resting on the bed in the prophet's chamber, he called Gehazi and said, "I must do something to show my gratitude to this man and this woman for their great kindness. Call the Shunammite woman, Gehazi." When she came into the room, Elisha said to her: "Madam, you have treated us with generous hospitality. Thou hast been careful for us with all this care. Now we would like to do something in return. Is there anything I can do for you? Would you like to make a request of the king, or the captain of the host?" But the woman answered, "I dwell among my own people. I have my comfortable home here and my husband. There is nothing that I desire from the king or the captain of the host."

When she had gone out, Elisha, perplexed and puzzled, said to Gehazi, "I wonder what we could do for her?" Gehazi was more discerning as to this particular situation than his master. He knew that there was one thing that this woman did not have, and which, like every good woman, she would rather have than anything else. So he said to Elisha, "This woman has no child, and her husband is old." Elisha thanked Gehazi for his advice and, wondering that he had not thought of it before, called the woman to his chamber again. When she came he made this announcement, "About this season, according to the time of life, thou shalt embrace a son."

In due season the promise was fulfilled and a child was born into that home in Shunem. His late arrival made him all the more precious to his father and mother. One day when he was following his father and the reapers in the harvest field, he had a sunstroke. "My head! my head," he cried, as his father held him in his arms. Calling a servant, his father did what is always the best thing to do. He said, "Carry him to his mother." His mother held him in her arms until noon, when he died. Then it seemed to her as if the bottom had dropped out of life. She almost wished that she had never had a child. Then she thought of Elisha. Taking the dead child, she carried him to the prophet's chamber, laid him on the bed of Elisha, and shut the door and went out. Then, ordering the servants to prepare and saddle one of the asses, she set out to find Elisha, who was at Mount Carmel. He saw her coming when she was yet afar off and said to Gehazi, "That, surely, is the Shunammite woman. I wonder if she is in any kind of trouble. Run to her, Gehazi, and say, Is it well with thee? Is it well with thy husband? Is it well with the child?" When Gehazi saluted her and asked these questions, she gave him a brief answer, "It is well." What was on her heart she could tell only to Elisha. As soon as she came up to where Elisha was standing, she dismounted from her beast, and kneeling at the prophet's feet, clasped his feet with her arms.

A Hard Heart

Gehazi did not like this action on her part, for it seemed to him unseemly that a woman should take such liberties with his master. He laid his hand on her shoulder and was about to thrust her away. But Elisha said, "Let her alone, for her soul is vexed within her, and the Lord hath hid it from me." The Bible can tell a great deal in two or three words. One stroke of the pen of inspiration sums up a man's character. That brief clause, "Gehazi came near to thrust her away," tells us a great deal about Gehazi. It lets us know that he was a man without native sympathy and pity and kindness of heart. He had no understanding of the heart's anguish and sorrow. Beware of such a man, and a hundred times more, beware of such a woman!

In brief sentences the broken-hearted mother told Elisha what had happened. It was he, God's prophet, who had given her the child. Now that the child was dead, could he not bring him back to life? Then Elisha did a very singular thing. He gave Gehazi his staff and told him to lay the staff upon the face of the child. Gehazi hurried off with the prophet's staff, and when he came to Shunem he went up into the prophet's chamber where the child lay dead and placed Elisha's staff across the face of the child. But it had no effect. "There was neither voice nor hearing."

Elisha's Staff

This, I suppose, is the only instance in the Bible where a miracle was attempted by or through a prophet, and the result was failure. Why was this attempted miracle a failure? Was it because the staff of Elisha lost its virtue when it passed out of the hands of a man of God into the hands of a man like Gehazi? Or was it because God would work the miracle only through the personal presence and touch of Elisha? Whatever the reason, Elisha's staff in the hands of Gehazi has occasioned great interest and no end of comment. One of the things often said, and truly, about this failure to work the miracle by absent treatment and through an intermediary or proxy, is that our best influence and our best work for God and for man will always be done by personal contact. You can write a check and send it to some worthy agency or needy family, but it will not do as much good as if you went yourself. You can give admirable directions and counsel, but it will not bring the same joy to you or to those whom you help, as if you spoke the word yourself. The staff method, although sometimes in the complexity of life it seems necessary, is always inferior to the personal method.

The sorrowing mother had no faith from the beginning in such a method, for she told Elisha that she would not leave him. He followed her back to Shunem and on the way met the returning Gehazi, who told him about his failure. "The child is not awake." Then Elisha went himself up into the chamber, and remembering the manner and method of his own great master, Elijah, stretched himself upon the child. When the child revived he called his mother and said to her, "Take up thy child."

Gehazi and Naaman

The next time we hear of Gehazi is in connection with Naaman. Naaman was the captain of the host of the King of Syria; "a great man with his master, and honorable, ... a mighty man in valor, but he was a leper." His leprosy was making rapid headway, and erelong would have terminated his life or driven him away from the king's court, had there not been in his household a Hebrew girl who had been taken captive. One day, knowing the sorrow of her mistress because of Naaman's leprosy, this little girl said, "Would God my lord were with the prophet that is in Samaria! for he would recover him of his leprosy." His wife persuaded Naaman to go to Samaria and try this cure. Nothing would be lost by it; perhaps this famous prophet could heal him. So Naaman, with a great retinue and with costly presents, ten talents of silver, six thousand pieces of gold, and ten changes of raiment, set out for Samaria.

Naaman did not like Elisha's reception of him, for instead of coming out to speak with him himself, he sent Gehazi; and still less did Naaman like Elisha's prescription, which was to wash in the Jordan seven times. But the better counsel of his friends prevailed. Naaman washed himself in the Jordan and his flesh came again as clean and fresh as that of a little child.

The grateful soldier and prince drove back all the way to Samaria to give thanks to Elisha and to confess his faith in the God of Elisha. Then he asked Elisha to let him bestow upon him a gift, some of the silver and gold and fine garments that he had brought with him. "I know, Elisha, that you yourself, a man of God, care nothing for these things; but you will be able to make good use of them. I have heard of your School of the Prophets. No doubt you need money to endow that school. Nothing would please me better." But Elisha refused to take a single silver or gold coin, or a single change of raiment. This was, first of all, because of his disdain for such things; and secondly, because he did not wish Naaman to get the idea that it was he, Elisha, who had healed him and not the God of Israel. Naaman then waved an adieu to Elisha, and driving down the steep roadway that leads from Samaria into the valley, set out for Damascus.

Gehazi's Lie

Gehazi had been a witness of the interview between Naaman and his master. His eye had caught the glitter of those gold and silver coins and the flash of those Syrian garments. He was utterly unable to understand why Elisha refused to take a present from Naaman. "What a fool," he thought to himself, "If he doesn't want it for himself, then why not take it and divide it among his followers and friends? I could make good use of some of that money myself." Quickly, the spirit of covetousness turned into resolve and action. "Behold," Gehazi said to himself, "my master hath spared this Syrian, Naaman, in not taking anything that he brought with him. But as the Lord liveth, I will run after him and take somewhat of him. He's nothing but a Syrian, anyway; a heathen and a foreigner; and I'll make hay while the sun shines."

His feet made fleet by avarice, Gehazi soon overtook Naaman, who when he saw him stopped his horses and got down from his chariot. Fearing that something had happened to his benefactor, Elisha, he said, "Is all well?" Then Gehazi told his crafty lie. Two of the young theological students had come to visit Elisha. Elisha had sent Gehazi to ask Naaman if he would give him for the benefit of these young men a talent of silver and two changes of raiment. There must have been a look of disappointment on the face of Naaman, and no doubt he wondered how Elisha could have changed his mind so quickly. But he pressed Gehazi, who probably needed little persuasion, to take two talents instead of one. The money was counted out into two bags, which were laid upon the back of two of the servants of Naaman, and Gehazi started back with them to Samaria. When he reached the city he took the men, not to the house of Elisha, but to the tower, some sort of a storehouse that he had. There he deposited the money and bade farewell to the servants of Naaman. Congratulating himself upon a good day's job and his smartness in hoodwinking both Naaman and Elisha, Gehazi went down to report to his master.

His Condemnation

When Gehazi came in Elisha said to him, "Whence comest thou, Gehazi?" Startled, but well controlled,

Gehazi replied, "Thy servant went nowhither." But Elisha, fastening his eye upon him, said, "Went not mine heart with thee, when the man turned again from his chariot to meet thee?"

We hear much in the newspapers today about an invention called the lie detector. When this device is connected with a witness, it gives, or is supposed to give, an infallible record as to whether or not he is telling the truth. If such an invention is really perfected, it will eliminate a vast amount of false witness in our courts, and will save the people vast sums which they pay for these prolonged and disgraceful trials. But ages ago Elisha had his own lie detector. He knew where Gehazi had gone, and what he had done. What a fool Gehazi was! How blind evil passion makes a man! After all this association with Elisha, the keen-witted Gehazi is nevertheless so dumb as to think that he can deceive the man of God!

As the guilty Gehazi, now speechless, stood before him, in words of burning indignation and scorn Elisha said to him, "Is it a time to receive money and garments, and the things that money can buy—sheep, and oxen, and menservants, and maidservants? When I am trying to call Israel to repentance and to bring the people back to God, have you no thought save of money and what it can buy? Liar! Hypocrite! Thief! You coveted the gold and silver of Naaman; now you have his gold and silver; but from this day forth you will have something else that Naaman had

—his leprosy!" And he went out from his presence a leper as white as snow. There, not far from Achan, and Ananias, and Judas, is his grave; and there is his epitaph, "A leper as white as snow."

Avarice

The epitaph on the grave of Gehazi, perhaps more than anything else in the Bible, save the bitter cry of Judas as he flung down the thirty pieces of silver at the feet of the high priest and scribes and Pharisees, "I have sinned in that I have betrayed innocent blood," shows the degrading effect of avarice and the love of money, which is the root of all evil. This is a vice which, unlike some other sins, grows stronger and develops with age. It warps the soul, turns good men into bad men, and prevents men of great capacity from becoming good men. Always its wages are the same—bitterness, disillusionment, and shame.

Love of Money Hides God

A man once came to visit Robert Hall, the famous English preacher, to take some exception to a statement the preacher had made in his sermon. Hall saw that the man was in the bondage of the love of money. Having truly sized the man up, Hall took a half sovereign out of his pocket, and opening the Bible pointed to the word, God. "Can you see that word?" he said to the man. "Certainly, I can see it," the man answered. Then Hall laid the half sovereign over the word. "Can you see it now?" he asked.

There was no need for the man to answer. It was an unforgettable sermon. Money, the love of it, can hide from the soul of man even the face of God. That was what happened to Gehazi.

Gehazi's sin was one of the worst recorded in the Bible, because it was the sin of a man who made use of his religious office and his pious association with the godly Elisha to get worldly profit. Gehazi has more successors than we commonly think. When religion is used as a cloak for ambition, or lust, or avarice, or lying, it is worse than infidelity itself. There are different degrees also in the Ancient and Dishonorable Order of Gehazi. Almost every church will have some members who make their appearance only when they have something to sell to the minister or to the church; and worse than that, Christianity is often wounded in the house of its friends by those who use their office or association in the Church to gain the confidence of people and, as Gehazi did with Naaman, "take something" from them.

A Warning to Religious People

Odious as he appears to us, it is nevertheless profitable for all who are in the Church and for all who have Christian associations to take a long look at Gehazi. When you look at him you realize the solemn truth that religious associations and even religious office and daily and constant contact with religious matters and with godly people cannot keep a man from sin. The only thing that will do that is what Christ said, "Watch and pray, lest ye enter into temptation."

How quickly everything can go wrong! The glitter of Naaman's gold and silver, Gehazi's sudden desire, the ready lie, the gold hid in the tower, the question of Elisha, the terrible sentence—in a single hour it was all over and Gehazi went out a leper as white as snow.

Standing by the grave of Gehazi, and reading that epitaph, "A leper as white as snow," one thinks of another "white as snow" in the Bible—"Though your sins be as scarlet, they shall be as white as snow." And that makes one think of Him who cleansed the lepers, and who can save us all from a leper's epitaph and the sinner's doom.

JOHN

VIII

"That disciple whom Jesus loved"

John 21: 7

A BEAUTIFUL and a wonderful epitaph. Five times it is recorded in John's Gospel. Some men prepare their own epitaphs. Benjamin Franklin prepared an epitaph that was never inscribed upon his tomb. John wrote his own epitaph, and yet this fact does not in any way invalidate the epitaph. It raises no doubt as to the beautiful truth of what he says. Charles Kingsley prepared this epitaph for the grave of his wife. "We love; we have loved; we shall love." All that, and more too, is summed up in John's briefer and more beautiful epitaph—"That disciple whom Jesus loved."

This is one of the most familiar sayings of the New Testament, familiar because of its tender beauty; and yet the more one meditates upon it, the more unusual, the more wonderful it seems. Here is the disciple whom Jesus loved. We know that he loved Lazarus as a friend, for the messengers who came to tell him of the sickness of Lazarus said to him, "He whom thou lovest is sick." Jesus perhaps on his human side had natural affinities, and among the Twelve Disciples it would not have been strange if there had been some who were personally more congenial than others. But far more than that is summed up and expressed in this celebrated epitaph —"That disciple whom Jesus loved."

Among these boys playing together on the shores of Galilee look earnestly into the face of this one, probably the youngest of the group. Peter, Andrew, James, and John. This is the one upon whom destiny has laid her hand, for men and churches and theologies will be named after this boy, and great buildings all over the world will rise as a memorial to him. Through the future ages he will be known and distinguished as "that disciple whom Jesus loved."

There are probably turning points in all our lives. Sometimes we can see and recognize those turning points and know when we have turned the point, and sometimes not. The turning point in John's life was that afternoon when he was walking with Andrew along the shores of the Jordan in the company of John the Baptist. Jesus passed by near them and the Baptist exclaimed, "Behold the Lamb of God that taketh away the sins of the world." Andrew and John were caught with that saying, and leaving the Baptist they followed Jesus at a respectable distance. Knowing that they were following him, Jesus suddenly stopped and turning said, "What seek ye?" They, perhaps embarrassed and for the lack of a better answer, replied, "Master, where dwellest thou?" Jesus said, "Come and see." They went with him, and that for John was the beginning of his wonderful association with Jesus. So firmly fixed was that event and that day in his mind that when he is an old man, perhaps half a century afterward, he is able to remember not only what happened and where it happened, but how high the sun was in heaven, the very hour of the day, for after he has related these events he adds, "It was about the tenth hour." That was the beginning of what we may call time's greatest friendship.

It does not satisfy us to think that this was a friendship just somewhat closer than that which existed between Jesus and the other disciples. Far more than that, we are sure, is bound up in this epitaph which John carved out for himself—"That disciple whom Jesus loved." If Jesus loved him, and in such a way as to warrant John, who is so modest as not to give his own name at all as the author of his Gospel, in recording such an epitaph, then there must have been special reasons for this special love.

I. Jesus Loved John Because John Saw Him and Believed in Him as the Divine Saviour

The thing that brought John to Jesus was that sermon by John the Baptist, "Behold the Lamb of God that taketh away the sins of the world." The whole Gospel is summed up in that sentence as a drop of dew takes in the whole glory of the sun in heaven. Christ likes to be taken and chosen and loved at his greatest. John did that. He took him as the Son of God, and the Lamb of God who was to be slain for the sins of the world. The redeeming love and pity of Christ goes out to all men, but there is another sense in which Christ loves men, and that is the way in which he loves the man who loves him as the only Saviour from sin.

II. Jesus Loved John Because of His Earnestness and His Zeal

In his famous painting of the Last Supper, which is really a great work, Leonardo has done full justice to all the disciples save John. His Judas and his Peter are truly masterpieces; but the John you see is a meek, unassuming, feminine looking creature, almost a simpering Mona Lisa. Certainly there is nothing in the sketch of John in the Four Gospels, or in the Book of Acts which suggests the character which has been produced by the brush of Leonardo. John was no weakling. He was a son of thunder.

There are two instances which show the great

earnestness and zeal of John. In both cases John suffered a rebuke; and yet the fault for which he was rebuked leaned to virtue's side. Mark tells us that after Jesus had preached a sermon on humility to the disciples, illustrated by a little child in his arms, John came to him and said that he and other disciples had seen a man casting out evil spirits in the name of Jesus and that they had forbidden him. No doubt it was John himself, or John and James, who did the forbidding. When Jesus heard this he rebuked John and the others, saying, "There is no man which shall do a miracle in my name, that can lightly speak evil of me. For he that is not against us is on our part." But even in John's presumptous rebuke to the man who was casting out evil spirits, there was a warm though mistaken zeal for the honor and the name of Christ which must have pleased Jesus.

The other incident was when a village of the Samaritans, immortal for its incivility, refused to receive Jesus. John wanted to call down fire from heaven and destroy the village and the people who lived in it. And once again he suffered a rebuke, for Jesus told him he knew not what spirit he was of, and lets him know very plainly such is not the spirit of the Master. Yet here again, it was a fault which leaned to virtue's side. Intolerance has back of it at least earnestness, and the trouble with the great multitude today is not intolerance, but indifference both to truth and to error.

Another example of John's great earnestness and zeal was the request which he made, together with James, for a seat at the right hand of Jesus when he came in the glory of his kingdom. One Gospel represents John's mother, Salome, as making this request. The other Gospel says that John and James made it themselves. At all events, they acquiesced in it, and it no doubt expressed their high ambition. From what John tells us of what transpired at the Last Supper, Jesus did honor him by giving him the seat next to him, and probably at his right hand, for he leaned on the breast of Jesus at the Supper. The other disciples were angry at John and James for making that request of Jesus, the chief seats, the right hand and the left hand, but there is nothing in the reply of Jesus to indicate that he himself was displeased with it. On the contrary, he takes John's extraordinary request very seriously and earnestly and explains to him and to James just what it involves—to be baptized with Christ's baptism and to drink his cup. He asked John and James if they felt that they could do this, and they answered unhesitatingly, "We can." Let it be remembered that Jesus did not rebuke them for this assurance. On the contrary, he must have rejoiced in it. James was the first of the Twelve Disciples to drink the cup of Christ and be baptized with the baptism of death when he was slain by the wicked Herod. John lingered long, longer than all the other apostles, but no doubt suffered martyrdom in the end. At least he had to all effects tasted the martyr's cup when, because he would not deny Christ and the Gospel, he was banished to the Isle of Patmos.

III. Jesus Loved John Because of His Courage and Loyalty

The only count against John in the Gospels is that he slept with the others in Gethsemane. But here, as with them, the spirit was willing but the flesh was weak. It was John who with the heart of a lion went into the courtyard and the high priest when Jesus was brought to trial that night, and not only went himself but spoke for Peter and had him admitted. Far better for Peter if he had not got in that night when he denied his Lord! But there was no denial by John. It may be an argument from silence, nevertheless it is a significant fact that John is the only one of the disciples who is spoken of as present at the Crucifixion. The daring love that brought him to the courtyard of the priest also brings him near to the Cross, so near that in his dying agony Christ can speak to him personally. The record is that he saw "the disciple whom he loved standing near." How that noble loyalty and courage of John must have warmed the heart of Christ and lighted up for him the last darkness. Had we been told only that John leaned on Jesus' breast at the Supper, we would know that he was an affectionate man and that he had the love of his Master. But when we are told that John also came as close to Christ as he could when he hung on the Cross, we learn that here is a love that knows no fear.

IV. John Loved Jesus Because of His Tenderness and the Love That Was in His Own Heart

Love only comprehendeth love, and knoweth whence it comes. That was beautifully true of John. If he is the apostle he tells us that God is love, and that God so loved the world as to give his only begotten Son, he is also the disciple who himself loved deeply and greatly. One example of the tenderness of John is that incomparable picture which he draws of the incidents of the Last Supper. "Now there was leaning on Jesus' breast at the supper that disciple whom Jesus loved." What a world of meaning is poured into that exquisite record! John was a strong, rugged man. He was a true son of thunder; and when we speak of him as the apostle of love, let it be remembered that not even St. Paul surpasses John in burning denunciations of those who hold low and false views of Christ and his Gospel. Yet with all his rugged strength and courage, John had that strain of tenderness in him without which no man is truly great. Here you can see it clearly in that lovely scene at the Supper.

Another instance of the tenderness of John is that moving scene at the Cross. Just before he tasted the last bitterness and gave up the ghost, Jesus looking down from the Cross saw his mother and John standing by. To his mother he said, "Woman, behold thy son," and then to John, "Behold thy mother." And from that hour, it is written, that disciple took her unto his own home. The last thought of Christ before his death was for the welfare and comfort of his mother; and it was to John that he commits his mother for the care and love which he knew John would bestow upon her.

These, then, I think, are the reasons why Jesus loved John; and these are the reasons why the Church loves him today. Because Jesus loved John, because he had these noble qualities—faith, earnestness, and zeal, courage, loyalty, and tenderness—Christ honors him by granting to him the glorious vision of the future triumph of his kingdom. It was John who saw the glory of Christ in the great vision on Patmos. It was John who was permitted to hear the great music of the Apocalypse; it was for John that a window was opened in heaven.

John, so far as we know, lived to a great age, and was the last of the Apostles to die. Some have interpreted that cryptic saying of Jesus in answer to Peter's curious question, "Lord, what shall this man do?" "If I will that he tarry until I come, what is that to thee?" to mean that until Christ comes again,

John, in his personality and in his Gospel, the Apocalypse, and his Epistles, will be the greatest witness to Christ. I do not think this interpretation, however interesting and suggestive, is the true one; but the long life that John lived on earth, so long that some indeed thought he would live until Christ came again, makes one feel that Christ let John stay on earth longer than any other of the Twelve Disciples in order that he might teach men what a true Christian is in faith, in life, and in hope.

Strive, then, to be a disciple whom Jesus loves. John was not a miracle, he was a man, a man of like passions with us, and he shows us what a Christian can be. Take John's Friend with you through life.

One of the most beautiful characters in English history and in English literature was Sir Philip Sidney, who fell on the battlefield of Zutphen, and who, dying and parched with thirst, pushed away the cup of water that another wounded man brought to him, saying, "Thy necessity is greater than mine." When one of Sir Philip Sidney's friends was dying he asked that this epitaph be placed upon his tomb: "Here lies Sir Philip Sidney's friend." "That disciple whom Jesus loved!" That is the proudest title that moral man can bear. Will it be your epitaph and mine?

ON THE GRAVES OF TWO YOUNG MEN

IX

"He departed without being desired"

II Chronicles 21: 20

"And they buried him; and all Israel mourned for him"

I Kings 14: 18

I HAVE no dread of a cemetery. Sometimes it is better to be there, and have fellowship with the dead who are buried, than to walk down the streets of our cities and meet the unburied dead; that is, those in whom faith and hope and love and purity have long been dead, leaving only the animal alive. In the cemetery the Bible of life is open and a passionless voice reads to us its great lessons and tells us to apply our hearts unto wisdom. Sometimes we can learn more from the silence of the dead than from the speech of the living. Whether it be a little churchyard, where under ancient elms the dead lie close to holy walls, or the dark spaces of some hoary cathedral, where the dead sleep under sculptured sarcophagus and lettered marble, or some wilderness battlefield where the nation has gathered the bodies of the soldiers who there gave their last full measure of devotion, or some rural hillside where the wind blows free like the viewless and intangible spirit which has returned to God who gave it, or some quiet acre by the banks of a river that flows silently and swiftly away like man's life—wherever it may be, the resting place of the dead has always something worth while to say to the living.

I like to read the epitaphs and inscriptions; an epitaph like that graven, with poetic license, of course, upon the tomb of Ann Rutledge in the pleasant Hilltop Cemetery near Petersburg on the Sangamon River:

"Out of me unworthy and unkown
The vibrations of deathless music;
'With malice toward none, with charity for all.'
Out of me the forgiveness of millions toward millions,
And the beneficent face of a nation
Shining with justice and truth.
I am Ann Rutledge who sleeps beneath these weeds,
Beloved in life of Abraham Lincoln,
Wedded to him, not through union,
But through separation.
Bloom forever, O Republic,
From the dust of my bosom!"

I like to rest near the yew tree in Stoke Poges and read Thomas Gray's fine tribute to his mother, in which he says that she was "the careful, tender mother of many children, one of whom alone had the misfortune to survive her." I have never seen it, but would like to see it, that inscription on the tomb of Charles Kingsley and his wife in Eversley Churchyard—"We love, we have loved, we shall love." Sometimes when I read bombastic and insincere epitaphs, I think that the one on David Hume's grave in Calton Hill, in Edinburgh, would be a good model: "David Hume, born 1711, died 1776, leaving it to posterity to add the rest." In a rural cemetery recently, in a pleasant country not far from here, I saw a little stone, and pushing back the leaves and vines, read this:

> "'Tis a little grave, but oh, have care,
> For world-wide hopes are buried there."

Sometime ago, wandering through one of the Old Testament cemeteries, there were two graves which caught my eye and held my interest. Both had been young men, both of them were sons of kings. One was Jehoram, the son of Jehoshaphat; the other, Abijah, the son of Jeroboam. That alone was interesting. But the strange thing was the inscriptions on these two graves. On the grave of Jehoram were these words, "He departed without being desired"; and on the grave of Abijah these words, "And all Israel mourned for him." At once I began to wonder about these two young men, both of royal blood, blessed, and alike in opportunity, both carried off in early death, but one so universally detested that none wept for him or wished him a day longer of life, and the other mourned over by an entire kingdom.

Let us pause first at this grave of the undesired and the unlamented young man with its strange epitaph, "He departed without being desired." Jehoram had a fine start in life, one of the greatest that any man could have, a great father. Jehoshaphat was one of the best of the kings of Judah. But, as we know from the case of Samuel, and from more recent examples all around us, the best of men may have the worst of sons. Train up the child in the way he should go, and when he is old he will not depart from it. That proposition still stands. Nevertheless, there are these exceptions, notable good men who had notoriously wicked sons. Sometimes, although the world may not discern it, there has been a weak place in the armor of the father. We know that Jehoshaphat's weakness was too great fondness for the company of the wicked kings of Israel. Several times this got him into trouble. Perhaps that former association led to the marriage of Jehoshaphat's son with a daughter of Ahab. Indeed, the ancient chronicler accounts for all the evil of Jehoram's reign on that score. He did evil in the sight of the Lord, the record tells us, because he had a daughter of Ahab to wife. Evil associations, as so often has been the case, corrupted good manners.

However, we can't blame it all on Jehoram's wicked wife. There was plenty of the strain of evil in himself. He celebrated his accession to the throne by murdering all his brothers. He was a cruel man, and of all the men to fear, he is the one to fear the most. There you have a fountain for all kinds of sin. He was an idolater, too. If he had set up a heathen shrine of his own and worshiped there, that would have been bad enough, but he did worse than that. Men are never satisfied to sin by themselves. Did you ever know a scoffer, or disbeliever in the Bible who was content to keep it to himself? Jehoram made others bow down with him before these unclean idols and made the people join in his acts of lust and licentiousness.

In the midst of his career of sin and crime Jehoram had a warning from the old prophet, Elijah. This time not a written message, but a spoken, perhaps because of the great age of the prophet. This grand old rebuker of royal sinners pronounced by letter a judgment upon the royal youth and told him because of his sins he would come to a speedy and disgusting death. This warning, however, did not stay Jehoram in his career of sin. At length he was smitten according to Elisha's prophecy with a disgusting disease and died a lingering death.

When the news got out in Jerusalem that Jehoram

was very sick, and probably could not get well, nobody was sorry. There were no anxious inquiries at the palace; none prayed for another day for the young king; nobody cried or sighed when his death was announced. There were no flowers as symbols of either real or formal affection or sorrow. No one, except those who had to go, went to the funeral; and there on his tombstone tonight you can read this terse, grim, laconic, terrible epitaph, "He departed without being desired."

It is easy to live so as to win such an epitaph. I have known men and women who departed without being desired. No one in the church felt badly; at the place of business there was no sense of loss, and even in the home there was a sense of relief. If any sorrow at all was felt, it was the sorrow over the death of what might have been, not what was. There is a well-worn path which leads straight out to the cemetery, to the grave upon which is written, "He departed without being desired." It is the path of cruelty, godlessness, impurity, selfishness, and conceit. There is an unpopularity which is a credit to a man, rather than otherwise. That Jesus had in mind when he said, "Woe to you when all men shall speak well of you." When Senator Vilas nominated Grover Cleveland for the presidency the second time, he swept the convention with his closing sentence, "We love him for the enemies he has made." Every good man ought to have some enemies. That is the proof that he was a man of principle and stood for something, and was not a reed shaken with the wind. That is an unpopularity to be coveted. Perhaps it is the greatest decoration that any man in this world can wear. But there is an unpopularity which is nothing short of terrible—the unpopularity won by self-indulgence, by disregard for the rights of man and the honor of woman, by irreverence for that which is high and holy. This is the unpopularity commemorated by this terrible epitaph, "He departed without being desired."

Now, let us turn to the other grave. Come and sit with me in the cool shade of this arbor vitae which bends low over the grave of the other young man, with its wonderful epitaph, "And all Israel mourned for him." Let me tell you the story of this young life.

> "The good die first, and they whose hearts
> are dry as summer's dust,
> Burn to the socket."

Sometimes; but not always; for in this case also the wicked die young. Nevertheless, it was a young man, and the good man, who died. The first thing that surprises us is that he was the son of a most wicked king, one of the worst, the man who made Israel to sin, Jeroboam. If I had read on the tomb of a son of a wicked king like Jeroboam that other epitaph, "He departed without being desired," I would not have been surprised; but here what I read on his grave, is this, "All Israel mourned for him."

With a wicked father and a mother not much better, heredity, home training, everyday example were all against Abijah, and the likelihood of his being a good man. According to all the rules of the present-day theories of heredity and psychology, he ought to have been a bad man. Yet here he is, without spot or stain, living in the wicked cesspool court of Jeroboam like a white lily amid the muck and mire of some marsh pond. I remember once noting with surprise and delight the red poppies blooming away up on the top of the mountains of Norway. If I had seen them on Flanders' Fields or in any of the low countries, it would have occasioned no surprise. But here one looked with pleasure and delight on the gentle, beautiful things growing there against the snow and the gray rugged broken rocks. So was the virtue of Abijah amid the vice of the court. Perhaps you think you might be a better Christian if you lived in another city, or had another occupation, or a different kind of superior for whom to work, or home environment more congenial and sympathetic. If so, remember this epitaph on the tomb of the young man who, although in a wicked land and in a wicked home, everywhere surrounded by idolatry and vice, yet lived so near to God that he won this epitaph on his grave, "All Israel mourned for him." The household of the Caesar in the days when Paul was a prisoner at Rome, that is, the household of Nero, was not a place favorable to the Christian life and virtue. On the contrary, it was a nest of crime and vice. Yet when Paul writes out of prison, he is able to say, "The saints of Caesar's household salute thee."

Unfortunately, this youth did not have long to live. Who is this woman disguised in the cloak and shawl of one of the peasants, going with a cruse of honey and ten loaves to visit the old man of God, Ahijah, at Shiloh, whom we see passing through the streets of the sacred town? It is none other than the wife of Jeroboam and the mother of this godly young man. Abijah has fallen sick. Trouble sends men to God, and even Jeroboam and his wicked wife turned to the man of God in their distress, hoping to learn, although in disguise, that their son would get well. Instead of that, the aged prophet announces his speedy death. But in contrast with the fate of his whole household, all of whom were to meet violent deaths and lie unburied, the young man was to die a natural death and sleep in a lamented tomb. We feel sorry for the disguised queen as she hurries back to the palace, only to be told as she goes up the stairway that Abijah is dead.

Since his death was sudden, the people had no opportunity to express their anxiety and friendly interest before his death. But as soon as the news got abroad there was universal regret and lamentation. There was great sorrow once in England at the time of the death of King Henry the Fourth's only son, Prince William, or the atheling, as the English fondly styled the child of their beloved Queen Mathilda. Returning from Normandy to England, the Prince with a number of nobles took passage in the White Ship, which lingered behind the rest of the royal fleet. When the vessel finally swept out to sea, it struck a rock at the mouth of the harbor and went down with all hands, leaving behind it only a terrible cry which echoed through the royal fleet. When the news reached the king, his father, he fell unconscious to the ground and rose never to smile again. All England, too, shared his grief over the popular prince. So, here, in ancient Israel, all ranks and classes wept for Abijah. Children were held up in the arms of their parents and told to imitate his life as his funeral cortège went by. In many a home there was sorrow as if for a child of their own. He had been so good and true and kind that when death struck him, it was not to destroy him, but only to spread abroad a fragrant memory of his beautiful character.

Both of these young men died an early death. You do not need to live long in order to do great good or great evil in the world. Jehoram did not live long, but long enough to do such great evil that he departed without being desired. Abijah did not live long, but long enough to make everyone in Israel feel sad when he was gone. In Rome one of the places I like the best is the Protestant Cemetery outside the gates, where John Keats is buried, and on his grave the words which he desired to be placed there,

> "Here lies one
> Whose name was writ on water."

But in a true sense, no one writes his name on water. Rather he writes it in characters which endure forever and spell the abiding influence of a good life or a bad life. We can afford to be careless at any other time of life rather than at the period of youth.

"In general, I have no patience with people who talk of the thoughtlessness of youth indulgently. I had infinitely rather hear of thoughtless old age and the indulgence due to that. When a man has done his work, and nothing can in any way be materially altered in his fate, let him forget his toil, and jest with his fate, if he will. But what excuse can you find for wilfulness of thought, at the very time when the very crisis of future fortune hangs on your indecisions? A youth depends on the chances, or the passions of the hour! A youth thoughtless! When the career of all his days depends on the opportunity of a moment! A youth thoughtless! When his every act is as a torch to the laid train of future conduct, and every imagination a fountain of life or death! Be thoughless in any years, rather than now—though, indeed, there is only one place where a man may be nobly thoughtless—his deathbed. No thinking should be left to be done there." [1]

Speaking once at a college commencement, as I entered the commencement hall, I saw books on sale which bore the name of a Samuel Morris, and pictures and a bust of him. As the commencement program went on there were occasional references to this young lad, Sammie Morris. When the exercises were over, I asked someone, "Who is this Sammie Morris?" He was a black boy, rescued from slavery in Africa, converted at a mission station, who made his way to New York on a sailing ship, and by interested friends was sent to this Christian institution. His heart was set on going back to Africa, but he was not long in college before he fell a victim to consumption. His life was short, his opportunities restricted, and yet in his life and after his death men paid tribute to the power of his faith. To the young men and young women of that institution he is an unfailing fountain of inspiration, and as they go out to all parts of the world to work for Christ they remember with gratitude this black boy whose grave today at Fort Wayne is hardly ever without a daily pilgrim and visitor.

The secret of the difference of Abijah's fate and of his different epitaph is contained in this record of him. "Because in him there is found some good thing towards the Lord God." What was that good thing?

[1] John Ruskin, *The Crown of Wild Olive.*

Not wealth or health or station. Not mere moral excellence, or talents, or attractiveness of personality, but something fundamental, something spiritual, of the heart. We know that in him this good thing was the fountain of his pure and godly life. He was a man of faith, not bowing to the idols of his father and mother. He knew that in our flesh dwelleth no good thing and had that contrition of repentance and faith of heart which God loves above all else. These are the things that count. This is the thing to covet. This is the touchstone of destiny, and the test of whether or not we have that good thing in our hearts is the answer we make to God as he speaks to us through the Cross of his Son, calling us to faith and repentance. Whatever honors may come to a man in this life, or wherever his name may be written by men upon earth, he who has in his heart that good thing toward God will have his name written in heaven, written in the Lamb's Book of Life.

DEMAS—HAVING LOVED THIS PRESENT WORLD

X

"Demas hath forsaken me, having loved this present world"

II Timothy 4: 10

THE family of the Greek merchant, Demetrius, are gathered in the garden in front of their red-roofed villa on the eastern shore of the Bay of Salonica. A marble stairway leads down to the boat landing where a galley is moored. In the distance can be seen the winglike sails of fishing craft. To the west, at the deepest recess of the bay, is the city of Thessalonica, named after the daughter of King Philip of Macedon. A Roman arch is plainly visible, and on the top of the hill back of the city the walls of the stadium. Across the bay, to the southwest, the snow on its summit turning pink and red under the last rays of the sun, rises the fabled abode of the gods, Mount Olympus. Coming down the graveled walk to the benches, where his family and friends are sitting by the shore of the bay, Demetrius thus addresses his daughter Damaris:

"Damaris, where is thy brother Demas? Why comes he not? It is a fortnight since we heard from him at Athens. The weekly galley arrived this morning, but he was not among the passengers. Tomorrow the races are held at the stadium. I have wagered a hundred thousand sesterces on the bay team which I bought for Demas at Antioch. Only Demas can drive this team, and without him the race is lost."

"Father," answers Damaris, "perhaps Demas is returning by land. He may have stopped at Thebes, or at Berea to visit old comrades of the school of rhetoric at Rhodes. But there is Nereus now!"

"Where, Nereus," said Demetrius, "is thy master? Why comest thou alone? No harm hath befallen my son, I trust."

"Here, sire, my master bade me give thee this."

Demetrius takes the roll of parchment, breaks the seal, and begins to read. As he reads a look of fear, disgust, and rage comes over his countenance.

"Hear, children of Demetrius," he cries, "Demas hath forsaken us! Demas hath abandoned his father, his mother, his brother, and his sister! He hath forsaken the gods! Demas hath become a Christian, a follower of the despised Crucified One, a disciple of that wild agitator, Paul, who was driven out of Thessalonica the last Ides of March! Hear what he writes:

"'Dear Father: Strolling ten days ago through the market place at Athens, where the philosophers and orators are wont to teach and to speak, I heard one speaking to a company who stood about him. He was altogether different from the rhetoricians and philosophers and players with words and babblers whom I have heard before. He seemed to speak with authority, and his words stirred deeply my heart. He spoke of God, of sin, of Eternal Life, and of one, Christ, who had died on the Cross, and in whom we have forgiveness and Eternal Life. When at the close he called for all those who would repent and believe to follow him, I went with him to his house. There I heard more about Eternal Life. Now I have become a disciple of the Way. I renounce the world of fashion and idleness and pleasure and wealth that hitherto I have known. Salute Andronicus, my brother, and Damaris, my sister, and my mother. One thing only I ask, father. Wilt thou for me manumit Nereus and my other slaves? All the rest of my possessions I leave with thee. Mourn not for me, father, for my heart is full of joy. I will pray that one day thou, with all our family, wilt find the Lord whom I have found.'"

That, or something like that, may have been the beginning of the Christian history of Demas. It was a bright morning. Alas, the clouds gather at the eventide. Here he lies buried, and here is his epitaph, one of the saddest of the Bible—"*Demas hath forsaken me, having loved this present world.*"

Paul was a man of intense feeling, and sometimes he could be quite sharp in his comments and his rebukes. When Mark forsook him on the first missionary journey and turned back at Pamphylia, Paul was so incensed that he would not take him with him on the next journey, and the dispute between him and Barnabas, Mark's uncle, over this matter led to their separation. But here Paul utters no word of censure or of blame. It is an epitaph of sorrow. "Demas hath forsaken me, having loved this present world."

Had it not been for this final mention of Demas by Paul, Demas would have gone down in history as a true and faithful follower of Paul and of Christ. Future ages would have thought of him in the terms in which he is mentioned in Paul's Letter to Philemon: "There salute thee Epaphras, my fellowprisoner in Christ Jesus; Marcus, Aristarchus, Luke, Demas, my fellowlaborers." Or, as he is mentioned in the end of the Letter to the Church at Colossae, "Luke, the beloved physician, and Demas, greet you." Demas appears here in high company, with such men as Luke and Epaphras and Aristarchus. A message from Demas warms the heart of Christians in far-off churches. Had this been all we knew about him, Demas would have been a name for young men's leagues; stained glass windows and marble sculptures would have described him. Churches would have been named the Church of St. Demas. Instead of that, this is all that we remember about him—"Demas hath forsaken me, having loved this present world."

After his conversion Demas appears to have been much in the company of Paul, no doubt following him on some of his long journeys in Europe and in Asia and across the seas. Although he is not named with Luke and Aristarchus as one of those who sailed with Paul on the shipwreck journey to Rome, he evidently thought so much of Paul and of the Christian faith that he joined Paul during his first imprisonment at Rome. Apparently, too, when Paul was brought back to Rome the second time, for the imprisonment which ended in his death, Demas was one of his companions. Thus far, everything is to the credit and high honor of Demas. Among all the friends of Paul you feel that you can count on Demas. Now, alas, at the very end Demas fails.

Did Demas begin to fear that he would share the fate of Paul? That Nero would put him to death too? Did he dread the lions of the arena, the torture, and the flames? Did the old life with its pleasures and its comforts come back upon him in this moment with resistless power? Did he begin to feel that he was too young, too intelligent, too well born, to suffer martyrdom like the other Christians? Did some sudden temptation grip him and bring him into the dust so that he felt ashamed to renew his association with Paul? We can only imagine what it was. But we can imagine, too, a scene that perhaps took place in the Mamertine dungeon. Luke, the beloved physician, appears at the gates of the dungeon one morning, and having been admitted by the guard, comes to the circular chamber where Paul is chained. We can imagine a conversation something like this:

PAUL: "Thou art welcome, Lucas, my son."

LUCAS: "I trust thou hast rested well, Paul, and that the medicine I gave thee for thy thorn hath eased somewhat its pain?"

PAUL: "Thou art skilful, Lucas, as a physician; but thou art better medicine to my soul than thou art for my body. After all, what matters now this thorn in the flesh, for the time is short, and I shall soon put off mortality. But, Lucas, why comest thou alone? Crescens, I know, has gone to Galatia; Titus I sent unto Dalmatia; and Tychicus I sent to Ephesus. But where is Demas? I sent him on no mission to any of the churches because I desired him to be with me until the end. No accident, Lucas, I trust, hath befallen Demas? The spies of Nero have not seized him? He is not sick, is he?"

LUCAS: "Father in Christ, I dread to tell thee—Demas hath forsaken thee. At the Appian gates last night Rufus and thy cousin Herodian met him as he passed through the gates going eastward. He sought to avoid them; but when they hailed him and asked him whither he was going, and how thou wast, he told them that he was giving up his Christian faith and was bound for his home at Thessalonica. I would have kept from thee this wound, Paul, but since thou hast asked me I must tell thee the truth."

PAUL: "Demas hath forsaken me! This present world! What power it has over the souls of men! I thought that I had broken its power over the soul of Demas, but now the world has claimed him again. Demas hath forsaken me, having loved this present world! Lucas, I will pray for thee that thou stand fast even unto the very end. Now, since Demas hath forsaken me, take thy parchment and write at once to Timothy in Ephesus. Tell him to come to me, and to come before winter, and tell him, Luke, to bring Mark with him, for he is profitable to me in the ministry. Once Mark forsook me and turned back; but through the grace of God we won him back again. Would that that had been the history of Demas!"

Of all the epitaphs on the graves of those who have backslidden from the Christian faith and have turned again to this world, the epitaph on the grave of Demas is the most embracing. It describes them all, whether it was fear of persecution, or fear of the loss of this world's goods, or the explosion of some long-subdued passion, this is the epitaph that tells their story, "Having loved this present world."

Standing over the grave of Demas and reading that epitaph, "Having loved this present world," there comes to mind the saying of a venerable follower of Christ, perhaps the oldest Christian then in the world, both in age and in the length of time that he had known and followed Christ. He had seen Christians of great promise dragged back into the world, and writing to young men he gives them this warning and counsel: "Love not the world, neither the things that are in the world. . . . . The world passeth away, and the lust thereof: but he that doeth the will of God abideth forever."

This is an epitaph which preaches its own sermon. The meaning of it is so apparent and so piercing that no one can miss it, and it warns us all to be on our guard against the seductive influence of the world in which we live, a world which is the natural and eternal enemy of Christ. It is not enough that the worthlessness of this present world should be demonstrated. We must have what the Scottish preacher, Dr. Chalmers, in a famous sermon called "the expulsive power of a new affection." If our love for Christ grows cold, any and every transgression, denial, betrayal, is possible. Watch and pray lest we enter into temptation.

"Sure I must fight if I would reign,
Increase my courage, Lord.
I'll bear the toil, endure the pain
Supported by Thy Word."[1]

There is a record of the name Demas appearing

[1] Isaac Watts.

among the politarchs, or magistrates, of Thessalonica. It is possible that when Demas renounced the Christian faith and returned to Thessalonica he was elevated to this office. As we used our imagination as to the beginning of the Christian life of Demas, now let us use it with regard to his life as a magistrate at Thessalonica.

In the crowded stadium on the top of the hill at Thessalonica, prisoners guilty of various crimes are brought before the box of the magistrate in the arena and sentenced to their fate—some to fight with a beast, some to the ax, and some to the flames. Now appears before Demas a man still in the morning of life. The moment Demas looks upon him he starts and a pallor comes over his face. It is none other than Crescens, his old friend and the friend of Paul. Hoping that Crescens will not recognize him, Demas asks the clerk for the charge against the prisoner, and the clerk answers, "An atheist; a destroyer of the gods; a Christian." Then Demas, turning to the prisoner in front of him, asks him the routine question, "Wilt thou swear by the image of Caesar? Wilt thou revile Christ?" Crescens answers, "I will not swear by Caesar's image! I will not renounce Christ, for he hath redeemed me from sin and from death." Demas replies, "If thou dost not repent and revile Christ, then I will commit thee to the flames or to the beasts of the arena." "I fear not the flames, neither do I fear the beasts," answers Crescens. "But, sir, thy face is familiar! Where is it that I have seen thee before? Thou art not Luke, neither art thou Aristarchus, neither art thou Tychicus, for he was thrown to the beasts at Ephesus. Now I know! Thou art Demas!"

"Yes," replied Demas. "Thou art right. It is Demas who is thy judge. As magistrate I must condemn thee, Crescens, to the beasts in the arena. But, Crescens, hesitate not. Hold fast to thy faith! Hold fast to thy Christ! The martyr's crown will soon be thine. Soon thou wilt be with Luke and Tychicus and Aristarchus, all that noble circle that used to meet at Rome. Soon thou wilt be with Paul himself. Would that thy fate, Crescens, were mine! Now I recall the words of our Lord which Lucas would sometimes read to us, 'What shall it profit a man, if he shall gain the whole world, and lose his own soul?' Peace, Crescens, eternal peace be with thy soul. But with me!"

XI

"He was eaten of worms, ... but the word of God grew"

Acts 12: 23

THIS epitaph is all the more striking and impressive because of what immediately precedes it. "The people shouted, saying, The voice of a god and not of a man." Then comes the epitaph, "He was eaten of worms."

Tonight we pause at the family burying plot of the Herods. A bad lot, these Herods. Both the name Herod and the sound of it suggests the law which in modern times has been called heredity, but which was declared ages ago when God gave the Commandments to Moses. In the second commandment God says that he is a jealous God, "visiting the iniquities of the fathers upon the children unto the third and fourth generations." Decendants of Esau, come to power in the century before Christ, the Herods showed that animalism, not unmixed with a certain pleasing generosity, which characterized the brother of Jacob who sold his birthright for a mess of pottage; but all of the Herods show evil and dangerous traits too.

Here lies buried the most famous of them, Herod the Great, who slew the innocents when Christ was born. He was also the murderer of his three sons. He drowned his brother-in-law, Aristobolus, and had his beautiful queen, Mariamne, whom he sincerely loved, strangled to death. When he lay dying in his ivory palace at Jericho, and knowing that people would rejoice rather than sorrow when they heard that Herod was dead, he had the representatives of the chief families shut up in the hippodrome, where they were to be put to death the moment the breath left his body. Thus he secured that there would be mourning in the land when he was dead.

Next to Herod lies his son Archelaus, banished by Augustus after nine years of misrule. And here is another son, Herod Antipas, also known as the Tetrarch. Herod Antipas was the Herod who, to please his wicked wife Herodias, beheaded John the Baptist. On the grave of Herod Antipas is that brief epitaph, written by Christ himself, "That fox."

Over there is Herod Agrippa, the one before whom Paul preached; and this is his epitaph written by himself, "Almost thou persuadest me to be a Christian."

Here is the grave of the bloodthirsty and beautiful

Herodias and her dancing daughter, Salome; and here is Bernice, the beautiful and profligate sister of Herod Agrippa; and by her side her sister, Drusilla, who married that Felix who trembled when Paul preached, but did not repent. A bad lot, all of them. Herod "the King," as he is called in the Acts, or Herod Agrippa I, was no exception in this family of profligates, degenerates, and murderers. On the grave of this Herod is written this epitaph: "He was eaten of worms, ... but the word of God grew."

Herod the King was a grandson of Herod the Great. As a young man he had spent much time in Rome and had been led into wild excesses by Drusus, the son of the Emperor Tiberius. A favorite of the Emperor Caligula, then of Claudius, this Herod was given sovereignty under the Romans in Palestine. In order to please the Jews, Herod instituted persecutions against the Christians. His first victim was James, the brother of John. "He killed James, the brother of John, with the sword." James and John had once asked Jesus that they might sit, the one at his right hand and the other at his left, when he came into his glory. When Jesus asked them if they were able to drink his cup and be baptized with his baptism, they said, We are able. Now James knows what that means. He was not the first of the martyrs, for that distinction belongs to Stephen, but the first of the Twelve Apostles to drink the martyr's cup.

When Herod saw that his crime pleased the people,

he sought to ingratiate himself further with them by laying his murderous hands upon an even more notable prisoner, Peter. Luke says that "when he saw that it pleased the Jews, he proceeded further to seize Peter also." The first act of sin suggests, sometimes demands, a second, and the second a third. "He proceedeth further" is the natural history of sin. When all hope had been given up and Peter's death seemed inevitable, the angel of the Lord awakened him and released him from the prison. The cruel Herod, when he could not find Peter, had all the soldiers who had guarded him put to death.

Then Herod went down to Caesarea. The people of Tyre and Sidon had in some way displeased him; but having bribed Blastus, the king's treasurer, they managed to secure peace with the king. Probably Blastus had told the people of Tyre and Sidon that Herod was very sensitive to flattery, and they proceeded to flatter him after his own taste. The narrative in the Book of Acts is supplemented by the graphic story of Josephus in his *Antiquities of the Jews.* Games and shows were being celebrated at Caesarea in connection with the victories of the Emperor Claudius in Britain. A great crowd had gathered on the second day of these spectacles. Herod came to the theater early in the morning arrayed in a gorgeous garment made wholly of silver. Standing before the people in the light of the morning sun, his garments shone with dazzling splendor. As they looked upon him and listened to his voice as he made them an oration, the people shouted, saying, "The Voice of a god, and not of a man!" Immediately he was stricken with a fatal disease.

When the people gathered around him, he said, "I whom you call a god am commanded presently to depart this life, while Providence thus reproves the lying words you just now said to me. And I who was by you called immortal am immediately to be hurried away by death." The Bible narrative, while not conflicting with that of Josephus, sums up the end of Herod in a much more concise and dramatic sentence: "And immediately an angel of the Lord smote him, because he gave not God the glory: and he was eaten of worms, and gave up the ghost. But the word of God grew and multiplied."

I. Divine Retribution

The first thing this epitaph on Herod's grave lets us know is that there is a law of justice and of retribution at work in the world. We cannot always see the working of that law; but now and then God lets us see the flashing of the sword of his judgments. The quick ending of Herod, one moment arrayed in silver and hailed as a god; the next hurled from his throne and the prey of worms, is one of those epiphanies and manifestations of judgment which let us know that right, after all, is on the throne, and that wrong will be punished and go down in darkness.

This epitaph is a brief philosophy of history. The history of the world is the judgment of the world. It always pays to read the chapter through to the end. If one had read only the beginning of this chapter, one would have seen Herod on his throne, a corrupt and irresistible tyrant. But when one reads to the end of the chapter, he sees Herod prostrate in the dust and eaten of worms, while the truth of God spreads and prospers.

Herod, apparently, is unrestrained in his evil doings, and goes from one wickedness to another, until we find him accepting the praise which belongs only to God. But that was the very hour when God smote him, just at the very climax of his infamy and splendor. It is often so in God's dealings with wicked men and wicked institutions in this world. He seems to permit them to do their will, and to the gaze and thought of man they seem irresistible and beyond the reach of judgment. Then God stretches out his arm. In his *History of the English People* Green relates the fall of Cardinal Wolsey, the man who said:

"Had I but served my God with half the zeal
I served my king, He would not in mine age
Have left me naked to mine enemies."

The career and fall of Wolsey is an example of how God permits wicked ambition to swell and advance until the hour of reckoning strikes. "Slowly," writes the historian, "the hand had crawled along the dial plate; slowly as if the event would never come; and wrong was heaped on wrong, and oppression cried, and it seemed as if no ear had heard its voice, till the measure of the wickedness was at length fulfilled. The finger touched the hour, and as the strokes of the great hammer rang out above the nation, in an instant the whole fabric of iniquity was shivered to ruins." That hour had now struck for Herod. It strikes for every doer of iniquity.

II. Christ's Cause Is Irresistible

The second thing that the epitaph on Herod's grave tells us is that right will finally prevail over wrong and the Kingdom of Christ over the Kingdom of Satan. This is an epitaph which can be read with satisfaction and comfort by all who believe in truth and who belong to the Kingdom of Christ. This epitaph, with its view of history, affords no little comfort, because it interprets the present. In Egypt Pharaoh gave his cruel order that all the male children of the Israelites should be destroyed. What power could resist such a monstrous edict? Only the fear of God in the hearts of those upon whom the despot counted to carry out his will. "But the midwives feared God, and did not as the king of Egypt commanded them, but saved the men children alive." Then came the second decree, that every son should be cast into the Nile. Who could circumvent this decree? Who but God, acting through the womanly compassion and the maternal instinct in the breast of Pharaoh's own daughter? When the grandfather of this same Herod, Herod the Great, heard of the birth of Jesus, the King of the Jews, at Bethlehem, he issued his ferocious decree that all the male children two years old and under be put to the sword. Thus he thought to destroy the rival king and stop the purpose of prophecy and of God. What power can now save the child Jesus from the bloody hand of Herod?

What but the power of God, who warned Joseph to take Mary and the child into Egypt? Then you come to that grand and dramatic sentence: "When Herod was dead, the angel of the Lord appeared to Joseph in Egypt, saying, Arise and take the young child and his mother and go into the land of Israel, for they are dead that sought the young child's life." Always that is the end of the conflict between enthroned wickedness and the representatives of righteousness. At the close of the battle comes this sentence, "They that sought the young child's life are dead." A helpless child against a cruel, bloodthirsty tyrant; but when we come to the end of the chapter, that is the final word—Herod dies, the child lives.

This world is a battlefield between Christ and Antichrist. Did we not have the great assurances of God, did we not have these luminous pages out of the book of the past, we might be tempted to despair of the final issue. If Satan is one day to be chained, he certainly is not chained today. Everywhere we see his ravages and the work of his servants. The curse of liquor, the infection of licentiousness, the exploitation of sex, the godless conception of government and of society, has reached a degree of power and of influence almost unprecedented in the history of the world. To the incarnate monarchs of materialism and of paganism and animalism an ever increasing multitude shout, "It is the voice of a god, and not of a man!" But we remember this Herod who was smitten by the angel of the Lord. We remember his grandfather who slew the children, but sought in vain to slay Jesus. We remember Pharaoh who sought in vain to destroy the destiny of God's people. We remember Haman who persuaded the Persian despot to issue a decree for the destruction of the Jews, but who himself perished on the gallows, sixty cubits high, that he had built for Mordecai, his Hebrew enemy.

One of the great things about Abraham Lincoln was that in the darkest days of the Civil War he never lost faith in the Republic or in the outcome of the struggle. One night, as he sat about the camp fire with Grant at City Point in March, 1865, and when it was apparent that the end of the Confederacy was not far off, Lincoln had been telling some of his characteristic anecdotes. At the end of one of his parables, Grant looked up and said, in his quiet way, "Mr. President, did you at any time doubt the final success of the cause?" "Never for a moment!" was Lincoln's reply, as he leaned forward in his camp chair and raised his hand by way of emphasis. Because we have the Bible with its exhibition of the justice of God and the repeated triumphs of righteousness, let us never doubt as to the final outcome, no matter how dark the present may seem to be.

"Workman of God! O lose not heart,
But learn what God is like;
And in the darkest battlefield
Thou shalt know where to strike.

Thrice blest is he to whom is given
The instinct that can tell
That God is on the field, when he
Is most invisible.

Blest too is he who can divine
Where real right doth lie,
And dares to take the side that seems
Wrong to man's blindfold eye.

For right is right, since God is God,
And right the day must win;
To doubt would be disloyalty,
To falter would be sin." [1]

[1] Frederick W. Faber.

WHEN THE ANGEL OF THE LORD SMITES

In this one-chapter history of Herod the King there is one of those tremendous contrasts of which the Bible alone is capable. When Peter was in Herod's prison, chained to two soldiers and guarded by sixteen, suddenly the prison was filled with light. "And the angel of the Lord . . . . smote Peter on the side . . . . and his chains fell from off his hands." The blow of the angel here was the blow of deliverance and liberty. It broke the chains asunder and set Peter free. When you come to the end of the chapter, the angel of the Lord appears again and once more lifts his arm to smite. But this time his blow brings judgment and death. "The angel of the Lord smote him, because he gave not God the glory: and he was eaten of worms, and gave up the ghost."

It was the same angel. It was the same outputting of the divine power. Yet how different the effect produced! In one place the blow of the angel set Peter free. Here it turns wicked Herod into corruption and death. God still sends forth his message and his messenger. But the Gospel upon different hearts can produce totally different effects. To those who resist it and deny it, it is as an angel of God who smites with condemnation and death. But to those who receive it, to those who believe it, it comes as the angel came that night in Herod's prison when he set Peter free. It illuminates with its light the dark places of life. It breaks asunder the chains of evil habit. It delivers us from the sentence of death and brings us into the liberty of the sons of God.

Does God Speak to Your Heart?

Such things happen to more men than Peter. Men lying in a dungeon deeper and darker than that of Herod have been set free by the angel of the Lord. It all depends upon the response we make. If we smite the hand that smites us, our chains remain on us and our prison becomes our tomb. But if we obey, as Peter obeyed when the angel touched him that night in Herod's prison, forgiveness and Eternal Life are ours.

Does the angel of God touch you? Does he speak to you? Does he warn you? Does he urge you? Has he touched your conscience, your heart? Then, like Peter, arise and follow him.

THE RICH YOUNG RULER

XII

"He went away sorrowful"

Matthew 19: 22

FOLLOWING his guide, Vergil, Dante came to the gate of hell, over which he read the words, "All hope abandon ye who enter here." Hearing sighs and lamentations and deep groans, he inquired of his guide who these might be, and was told that they were the souls who had lived without praise or blame, who did not rebel against God, nor yet were true to him, but were for themselves only. Mercy and justice both scorned them. Heaven would not have them, and hell rejected them. Therefore it was that Dante found them here at the gates of hell. A whirling flag passed by him, followed by a long train of spirits, and among these Dante recognized "the shade of him who through cowardice made the great refusal." By some this shade has been identified as the Rich Young Ruler who turned away from Christ and went away sorrowful.

Tonight we visit that corner of the biblical cemetery where lie buried those who turned away from Christ—Pilate, Judas, Demas, Agrippa, Felix, and the Rich Young Ruler. The epitaph on his grave is one of the saddest in the Bible—"He went away sorrowful." All three evangelists, Matthew, Mark, and Luke, are careful to record the fact that he went away sorrowful. There was something in the look of this young man when he turned away from Jesus which haunted the disciples, and has haunted the world ever since.

The threefold account in the Gospels of the Rich Young Ruler is an interesting example of how one Gospel supplements the other. Matthew tells us that he was a young man; Luke tells us that he was a ruler; and Mark tells us that Jesus, looking upon him, loved him. Thus we have the composite portrait of the Rich Young Ruler.

I. The Attractiveness of the Young Man

Mark says that Jesus, looking upon him, loved him. All who have looked upon him have felt the same way. Undoubtedly, there is something winsome and attractive in this Rich Young Ruler, something about him which holds our attention; and the interest in him is increased, although saddened, by the fact that he went away sorrowful. What are some of the things in this young man that Christ admired, and which makes us admire him after all these centuries?

Enthusiasm

In the first place, the young man was full of enthusiasm. Mark, always the graphic historian, relates what Matthew and Luke do not tell us, that the young man ran to meet Jesus and kneeled before him when he asked him his great question about Eternal Life. I heard of a grave somewhere on which was this epitaph—"He was an enemy of enthusiasm." There are not a few living, as well as dead, enemies of enthusiasm. But without enthusiasm nothing good and great has ever been accomplished. Napoleon said that men of imagination rule the world. We say the same thing when we say that men of enthusiasm rule the world. David Livingstone in one place says, "I find I wrote [he was speaking of new rivers he had discovered] when the emotions caused by the magnificent prospect might subject me to a charge of enthusiasm; a charge which I deserved, as nothing good or great has ever been accomplished in the world without it." Without enthusiasm no battles have been won, no Iliads written, no cathedrals builded, no empires founded. Some would permit enthusiasm in every life, but exclude it from the highest field of all, the welfare of the soul. This young man was enthusiastic about his soul and its welfare. That in itself makes him unusual.

Courage

We like his courage, too. Nicodemus also was a ruler of the Jews like this young man, but he came to

Jesus by night, apparently at first, at least, not having the courage to come and talk openly with Christ. But the Rich Young Ruler ran out on the street, in plain sight of everybody, and fell at the feet of Jesus. This was the more remarkable because he belonged to the ruling class of the land, the Pharisees, who looked with such disfavor upon Jesus. Therefore when he came to him and asked him this question he showed that he had the courage and the sense to overcome the natural prejudice of his class and ask spiritual advice from one whom they scorned.

Ambition

The young man showed a deep interest in the highest things. He wanted to make the most of his life and was not satisfied with just the ordinary attainments and standards. In Rugby Chapel, the noble tribute to his father, commenting on the nothingness and purposeless existence of a great number of men in this world, Matthew Arnold says:

"What is the course of the life
Of mortal men on the earth?
Most men eddy about
Here and there, eat and drink,
Chatter and love and hate,
Gather and squander, are raised
Aloft, are hurled in the dust.
Striving blindly, achieving
Nothing; and then they die,

Perish; and no one asks
Who or what they have been,
More than he asks what waves
In the moonlit solitudes mild
Of the midmost ocean, have swelled,
Foam for a moment, and gone."

But in contrast with this majority:

"There are some whom a thirst,
Ardent, unquenchable, fires,
Not with the crowd to be spent,
Not without aim to go round
In an eddy of purposeless dust;
Effort unmeaning and vain."

A young man who has an enthusiasm for something else than just the ordinary sports and pleasures of youth is a great asset to the Kingdom of God, and wherever you find him he is the chosen and elect in the army of the Lord.

Unspotted from the World

This young man had kept himself unspotted from the world. Up to his light, he had kept the Commandments, and when Christ asked him about a number of the Commandments, he could truthfully say that according to his light and standard he had kept them from his youth up. This again marks him as an exceptional young man. John B. Gough, the great temperance orator of two generations ago, died while delivering one of his famous lectures. His last sentence was this: "Young man, keep your record clean!" This is what this young ruler had done, and that was one of the reasons why Jesus loved him.

The particular Commandments about which Christ asked him were the following: "Thou shalt not commit adultery," "Thou shalt not kill," "Thou shalt not steal," "Thou shalt not bear false witness," and "Honor thy father and mother." The young ruler had no conception of the high spiritual interpretation of the Commandments as Christ interprets them in his Sermon on the Mount. But even in the external sense of which the young ruler was thinking, what a different world we would have if we had more young men of his age who could answer concerning those five Commandments as he did!

Desires Eternal Life

The young man had a thirst for Eternal Life. This world had not altogether hidden from him the other world. As for this world, he had every reason to be satisfied with it. See what the world had given him: the most honorable public station and office, a ruler in the synagogue; and with that, social standing and rank; and with that great riches. That combination generally suffices to stifle all spiritual desire in the heart of man. But this young man was an exception. He hungered and thirsted for something else. He probably had heard Christ speak on the subject of Eternal Life, and what Jesus said struck an answering chord in his breast. These, then, are the qualities which made this young man notable and worthy of the love and admiration of Jesus.

II. The Searching Test

When the young man, in answer to the question of Christ, said, and evidently with an air of disappointment, as if he had expected Christ to tell him something else, "All these have I kept from my youth up," Jesus, looking upon him, loved him, and then put him to the supreme test, "One thing thou lackest: go thy way, sell whatsoever thou hast, and give to the poor, and thou shalt have treasure in heaven; and come take up the cross, and follow me."

There is no ground for the theory which is somehow inferred from this incident, namely, that Christ here disavows for all his disciples the right of personal property. This is absurd, in the first place, because Christ told the young man to *sell* his possessions. He did not tell him to give them away, as if he had no right to them, but told him to *sell* them; and thereby he recognized one of the great human rights, the right to personal property; and where that right is recognized you will have the highest civilization. If all were sellers, it is well to remember that there would be no buyers.

In the second place, it is clear from his dealing

with other disciples that Christ did not make giving up all property a universal condition of discipleship. There was Zaccheus, for example. Zaccheus was a rich man, and as a publican he had probably gained his wealth in questionable ways. Zaccheus as much as admits that when he says that he will give half of his goods to the poor, and if he has wronged any he will restore unto him fourfold.

But Christ did not tell Zaccheus to sell all that he had. Another case in point was that of the man who claimed to have been wronged by his brother, and asked Christ to compel his brother to make restitution. What did Christ say? "Man, who made me a divider over you?" Instead of entering into a personal dispute over property, Jesus warned the man against covetousness. If Christ had been talking to Nicodemus, instead of this Rich Young Ruler, perhaps he would have told him, if he would be a disciple, to get rid first of all of his fear of the opinion of other Pharisees. Had he been talking to Herod Antipas, or had Herod asked Jesus, "What must I do to inherit Eternal Life?" Jesus would have told him, "Go and put away thy brother Philip's wife." The main thing is that in the case of this Rich Young Ruler it was his trust in riches which stood between him and following Christ. The test was too much for him. His countenance fell at the saying. The eager light that had been in his face faded away.

When he heard these things, Luke says, "He was exceeding sorrowful, for he was very rich."

III. The Sadness of His Failure

The main thing in this narrative is not the particular thing that made the young man turn away from Christ, but the fact that he did turn away, and that he went away sorrowful. This will always be so.

There was the sorrow, first of all, of deep disappointment. He had an earnest and sincere desire for Eternal Life, and did not doubt that Christ knew the way to Eternal Life. But when Christ told him what he must do, he was not ready to pay the price. Therefore, his deep disappointment, not only in the answer of Christ, but in his own inability to respond to that answer. He was sorry because he had made a sudden discovery that he was not all that he had hoped he was, or thought that he was. He had never imagined that his riches, or his trust in riches, stood between him and that which he had always regarded as first, Eternal Life. There is such a thing as disappointment in others, but deeper and sadder is the disappointment in yourself.

Again, there was the sorrow of inner disquietude and regret. If the young man had gone away in a rage, the way Naaman did when Elisha told him to wash in the Jordan, or the way others have done when asked to make the necessary sacrifices, I do not imagine that the writers of the Gospel would have thought his story worth preserving and recording. But the Holy Spirit has preserved it for us because here was a young man who went away *sorrowful.*

I wonder what his subsequent history was. Recently I received a letter from a man who had seen the announcement that I was to preach on this text. In the letter he expresses the hope that I will be fair and just with this young man, and go on the assumption that he probably afterward changed his mind, sold his possessions, gave all to the poor, and took up his cross and followed Jesus. I, too, would like to believe that; but there is nothing in the record which gives us any ground for such a belief. The Gospels are silent as to his history after he left Jesus, and the last we see of him is that sorrowful look on his face when he turned away from Christ. To do wrong impulsively, in anger, or in passion is one thing, and brings its retribution; but it is another, and a far sadder, thing when a man knowingly and deliberately, although sadly, turns away from Christ.

Memory and Regret

I find nothing in the Gospels to justify the picture of this young man coming back to Christ, for I believe that this was his great moment; that when Christ spoke to him he was not far from the Kingdom of God. Then he could have entered the gate, but he refused and went away sorrowful. I can, however, imagine something else about this Rich Young Ruler.

I can imagine him long years afterward, with his riches, which were great even when he was a youth and first met Christ, now greatly increased and multiplied, surrounded perhaps by a numerous family, and saluted when he passed down the streets of the city as a man of distinction and worthy of all honor. But one day, perhaps an old record in one of his books or accounts, or the passing glimpse of the face of one whom he had known as a follower of Jesus, suddenly brings him back to that memorable day on the highway near Jerusalem when he ran and fell at the feet of Jesus and asked him the way to Eternal Life. Sadly he contrasts the eager, impulsive, enthusiastic youth of the long ago with the present world-sated self. With a sigh he said, "Then, if I had followed Christ, I might have had Eternal Life—but now!"

Be sure of this: no disciple of Christ ever ceased to follow him and felt happy over it. No one ever dropped out of the Christian life, turned away from Christ and the Bible, and got any joy out of it. Equally true is it that no one ever felt moved to follow Christ, to be his disciple, or was almost his disciple, and yet turned away from him without knowing the sorrow that this young man did when he made the Great Refusal and turned his back on Christ.

Can You Pay the Price?

Do any of us see ourselves in the situation of this lovable young man? What is it, what will it be, that stands between you and Christ? With one, is it a companionship or affection? With another, the love of this present world? With another, an appetite, a habit, or a desire? But whatever it is, be sure of this: when you go away from Christ you go away sorrowful. Away from him is away from joy and from peace.

If you are hesitating tonight, if you have a secret yearning for Christ, and that means for Eternal Life, for something greater and better than you are, and yet feel the pull of something within you, or something or someone upon you, that holds you back, then pause for a little and meditate by this old tomb in the Bible graveyard. Get down on your knees and remove the grass and the weeds that half obscure the inscription on the stone. When you have done that then you can make out the following inscription and epitaph:

"Here lies the *Rich Young Ruler*—
He lived a moral life;
He kept the Commandments.
He ran to Jesus, and
Asked for Eternal Life.
Jesus loved him and told him
To take up his cross
And follow Him;
But he went away sorrowful."

FELIX

XIII

"Felix trembled"

Acts 24: 25

THAT is the epitaph upon the grave of Felix, the governor of Judea, before whom Paul pleaded his case. Felix trembled, but he did not repent. Felix was a victim of tomorrow. If today has slain its thousands, tomorrow has slain its tens of thousands.

> "Tomorrow, and tomorrow, and tomorrow,
> Creeps in this petty pace from day to day,
> To the last syllable of recorded time;
> And all our yesterdays have lighted fools
> The way to dusty death."

Felix trembled, but said Tomorrow, when God, speaking to his conscience through the voice of the Apostle Paul, said, Today. The Bible delights in striking contrasts. It gives us Abel and Cain, the types of innocence and guilt, standing before the altar of God; Elijah and Jezebel; Jacob and Esau; Jesus and Pilate; Judas and John at the Last Supper; and here today in the palace of the governor at Caesarea, Paul and Felix. What a contrast! On the throne sat Felix, the faded and withered pagan. A former slave, he became a favorite of Claudius, and by that emperor was exalted to high rank. Greed, cruelty, and lust were stamped upon his countenance. His administration as Procurator of Judea had been marked by injustice, extortion, and violence. By his side sat the lovely Jewess, Drusilla, a daughter of Herod Agrippa. She had first married a Gentile, who, to please her, had become a Jew. Then Felix, with the aid of a sorcerer's incantations, had won her from her husband, and was living with her in sin and shame. All that was dishonorable in mankind was represented by that combination of Felix and Drusilla as they sat on the throne awaiting the address by St. Paul. Before them, with chains on his arms, and his body scarred with the marks of his sufferings for Christ's sake, and his coarse garment which his own hands had woven contrasting with the velvet and purple of Felix and his paramour, stood the lonely ambassador for Christ.

While waiting for a formal charge against St. Paul, and more information about him, Felix thought it would be interesting to hear Paul speak; and since Drusilla was of Jewish race and would be interested in this famous Hebrew preacher and agitator, Felix invited her to come with him to the audience chamber.

The responsibility of every preacher is great. Great because he has a solemn truth to proclaim, the Everlasting Gospel; great because he may never preach again, and great because those to whom he is preaching may never hear him or any other preacher again. Therefore, like Richard Baxter, he ought ever to preach

> "As never sure to preach again,
> And as a dying man to dying men."

Great was the responsibility of Paul on this occasion. How easy it would have been for him to tone things down in the presence of his distinguished auditors. How easy for him to have preached on vague generalities or harmless platitudes, or to have bestowed upon Felix and his mistress fulsome flattery and hollow eulogy, but with Paul it was always, "Woe is me, if I preach not the gospel!" Instead of flattering his distinguished audience, he told them of their sins and of the great realities of righteousness and the life to come. One of the court preachers, standing before a corrupt French king, commenced his sermon by saying, "Sire, I have not come here to flatter you. I find no grounds for doing so in the gospel." So this ambassador in chains wastes no words in flattery, but preaches the truth of God to

Felix and Drusilla. It is one thing to preach *before* a congregation. It is another thing to preach *to* a congregation. Paul was the kind of preacher who preached *to* and not *before* a congregation.

I. The Sermon and Its Effect

Paul's sermon had three heads. He reasoned with Felix of righteousness, temperance, and judgment to come. Paul was a great reasoner, a great intellect and logician, as well as a great heart. None ever reasoned of Christianity as he did. Christianity is the most reasonable thing in the world, and those who preach it ought to know how to reason concerning it, and their great model in this respect is St. Paul.

The first head of the sermon was Righteousness. Paul struck the chord of righteousness and justice which underlies the universe. Righteousness and judgment are the habitation of God's throne. The order of the universe is moral. The stars in their courses are fighting against Sisera and all his hosts, even when to our imperfect vision it seems that truth and righteousness have no advocates and friends. When Paul began to reason about righteousness, I have no doubt that Felix and Drusilla looked at one another in surprise. That was not the kind of sermon they were expecting. Perhaps they were looking for just a half hour's entertainment, and thought that Paul would hold forth on the relationship of

Christianity to Judaism, or some mysterious subject, such as predestination, or the resurrection of the dead. But instead of that Paul talked to them about righteousness. No dates are numbered, no places given, no names pronounced; but the sermon Paul preached uncovered the past of Felix. He thought of the bribes he had paid and received, of innocent men he had cast into prison, of people in the streets who had been run down by his soldiers, of homes and towns made desolate and laid waste at his command. When he had done these things he had no compunction of conscience. It was the custom of the day. But now, as Paul preaches about righteousness, that terrible past rises before him in fearful resurrection and accusation.

Felix and Drusilla have not recovered from their astonishment when Paul launches out on the second head of his sermon, Temperance, or self-control. Now their faces blanch, as conscience points the finger and says to Felix, "Thou art the man," and to Drusilla, "Thou art the woman." Drusilla is decidedly uncomfortable. She thinks of her shameful escapades, of the husband she had abandoned, of her adulterous union with Felix, of the rumors about her relationship with her own brother. Instead of hearing a sermon about the relationship of Christianity and Judaism, something upon which she, as a Jewess, might have made a comment, what she heard was a sermon on the seventh commandment, "Thou shalt not commit adultery."

Both Felix and Drusilla now wish they had never seen this preacher at all. I can imagine Drusilla saying, "Why don't you stop this fool? Why did you bring me here to listen to such a harangue as this? Is this my lord's idea of an entertainment?" And Felix answered, "I had no idea that he would speak in such a fashion. I would like to stop him; and yet, I dare not, for the voice of a god seems to be speaking through him."

Paul then comes to the thrilling climax of the sermon, Judgment to Come. That is a subject that is left out of most sermons today. But Paul did not leave it out. The Bible does not leave it out; Christ does not leave it out. It is easy to say that we know nothing about what happens after death, that souls cannot be won to the Kingdom of God in that way, and that it will not do to frighten people, or try to frighten them, by a future judgment. Therefore let us confine ourselves to this life and its duties, and leave the future to itself. But Paul was preaching not only to the times, but to the eternities. Like the preaching of his Master, who spoke as ever standing under the cope of another world, Paul reasoned with Felix of judgment to come. He tells him and his paramour that this life is not all; that although a wicked man may have his fine clothes, his good times, his women and wine, his chariots and villas in this world, he may be cast into hell in the next, for we must all stand before the judgment seat of Christ.

Paul made Felix see that judgment throne, and when he saw it, Felix trembled. Seldom, if ever, has preaching registered such a triumph as that. Felix is the last man one would expect to tremble. He had listened in his day to all kinds of orators, enthusiasts, mystics, and philosophers; but never had he trembled until he heard Paul preach of righteousness, temperance, and judgment to come. The purpose of preaching is not to make people comfortable, to cast them into a moral stupor, to fill their mind with illusions, but to awaken their conscience. This is what the word of God, which is quick and powerful, sharper than any two-edged sword, a discerner of the thoughts and intents of the heart, did to Felix. It awakened his conscience; it made him tremble. Man is first, and above all else, a moral being. He has a conscience. And even in the worst of men, Felix, Pilate, and Judas, that conscience can be awakened. Felix trembled. This, I say, was one of the greatest triumphs that a preacher ever had. Felix trembled! What a grand demonstration of the fact of conscience and the power of the preached word of God!

II. A Lost Sermon

It was a great triumph of preaching when Paul made Felix tremble. Yet at the same time it was one of the greatest recorded failures of a sermon. Felix trembled, but he did not repent. The reason for this failure was not in the message or the preacher, but in the man who heard the sermon. Nothing was accomplished. The preacher had brought Felix to the gates of repentance, but he would not go in. If, as some think, every soul has its guardian angel who attends it during its earthly probation, and watches anxiously over it as it passes through its crises, how then the guardian angel of Felix must have grieved as he saw his mortal charge so near to the gates of repentance only to turn from them and plunge deeper and deeper into sin. Instead of repenting and crying out, as did the Philippian jailer, "Sir, what must I do to be saved?" Felix brought the sermon to an end by saying, "Go thy way for this time. When I have a convenient season I will call for thee." So he passes from the stage of the New Testament drama, a man who trembled but was lost, a man who was almost persuaded but went back, a man who knew the truth but would not do it. If Christ saw with sorrow the rich young man who was not far from the Kingdom go away from him, what must have been the sorrow of Paul as the soldiers led him out of the audience chamber that day, for Paul knew that he had touched the heart and conscience of Felix with that sermon on righteousness, temperance, and judgment to come. Back into the world went Felix, the memory of the sermon disturbing him perhaps from time to time, but the word of the preacher growing feebler and feebler, until it was forgotten and lost altogether in the business diversions, the pleasures and the lusts of life. Felix was a victom of Tomorrow.

III. Lost Opportunity

All the great opportunities of life are opportunities of today and not of tomorrow. To say tomorrow to them, as Felix did, is to say goodbye to them.

This is true of the opportunity for education, for fitting one's self for a worthy place and office in life. The man who says, "By and by, when I have a more convenient season, when I feel more like self-denial, then I will apply myself and store the mind with knowledge," awakes to find that today has passed and the next day is still tomorrow. This is true also of acts of kindness, of words of appreciation, of ministries of affections. They have their Now, their Today, and to say, "When I have a more convenient season" to these great opportunities is to bid them depart from you.

"I did not know how short your day would be!
I had you safe, and words could wait awhile—
E'en when your eyes begged tenderness of me,
Behind their smile.

And now for you, so dark, so long, is night!
I speak, but on my knees, unheard, alone—
What words were these to make a short day bright—
'If I had known! Ah, love—if I had known!' "[1]

So to opportunities to fit ourselves for usefulness, for kind and tender ministry to those who soon will be beyond our ministry, to the appeal of conscience, to the demand of repentance, we say, "Go thy way for this time. When I have a more convenient season I will call for thee."

Solemnly true is this of the greatest of all opportunities, the opportunity which comes to a man when the Holy Spirit speaks to his heart and calls upon him to repent and believe in the Lord Jesus Christ. To say Tomorrow when God says Today may mean farewell to God. The first reason for this is that no man is sure of tomorrow. We know not what a day may bring forth. Tomorrow quickly becomes yesterday. Nothing is so fragile as our hold upon life. It is easy for us to think all others mortal but ourselves. But who of us knows that he will be here next week? In the midst of life we are in death. The only time that belongs to us is Today, not Tomorrow. Now, not Then!

The second reason why it is always dangerous, and sometimes fatal, to say Tomorrow when God says Today, is that the impression which is made today on

[1] Ruth Guthrie Harding.

the soul and conscience may vanish by tomorrow. Impressions and emotions are good, but they are not enough. "Saw I not thee with him in the garden?" said one to the denying Peter in the courtyard of the high priest. Emotions are not enough, for the heart is fickle and deceitful above all else.

In imagination you can follow Felix after he had dismissed Paul, telling him that he would call for him at a more convenient season. For a little time, no doubt, the impression Paul had made remained with Felix. He did not seem quite himself as he engaged in the games that night, nor did he seem to take just the same delight in the voluptuous charms of Drusilla, nor did the theatrical shows engross him as formerly they had done. But the next day his discomfort was not quite so keen, and the next day still less so; and within a short time Felix was himself again, his old sinful, sensual self, not that real, true, divine self which Paul for a moment had raised to the surface by the mighty lever of his preaching.

How many there are who repeat the moral history of Felix. Oh, if the history of this, or any church like it, where the Gospel has been preached, could be written! What if the stones should cry out of the wall and the beam out of the timber should answer them, what a story they would tell of those whose conscience was stirred, whose heart for a moment was softened, and who were almost persuaded to turn from their sinful paths and seek pardon and life eternal in Christ. They were just between the winning and the losing; but instead of coming they said, "Some other Sunday. When I have a more convenient season, when I can think the subject over more leisurely, then I will decide and act. So they passed out into the deep and dark night of rejection of Christ and Eternal Life. *Then* they were near to the Kingdom; now none is farther from it. If we resist the highest impulses when they speak within our souls, they come not back with the same force and power. Light rejected may become darkness. That was what Jesus meant when he said, "Take heed that the light in thee shall not become darkness." Felix, Luke tells us, heard Paul preach frequently after this first dramatic meeting. He sent for him often and "communed with him," but there is nothing to indicate that Paul ever again made Felix tremble. That was his opportunity, and Felix let it pass.

The only convenient season is God's season. Clement L. Vallandigham, the eloquent, powerful, and somewhat notorious "Copperhead" and opponent of Lincoln's administration, came of godly parents, his father being the pastor of the Presbyterian Church at Lisbon, Ohio. Although he was the subject of so many prayers, and had before him daily the example of true Christian living, Vallandigham deferred till well along in life a profession of faith in Christ as his Saviour. In a beautiful letter written in 1855 to his brother, he pays an eloquent tribute to his godly home and his saintly father and mother, and then says, "Yet in all this have I not seen God visibly, palpably, seen and felt him as my God and Redeemer. Religion has ever been to me a thing belonging to the future, a something some day to be sought after, certainly to be sought after, but tomorrow. That tomorrow never came: there was no such thing in all God's creation to come; and I knew and realized it not these many years. Fool that I was! Tomorrow was ever one day in advance. Yesterday, this day, was the morrow. It came, but it was no longer tomorrow, but Today with all its terribleness, and it was all that belonged to me."

Would that all could realize the truth that tomorrow is no longer the morrow when it comes, but only today!

A man once dreamed that he was standing in the midst of a great conclave of the infernal spirits, with Satan, their lord, sitting over them upon his throne. The archenemy of mankind was seeking some new way in which he might beguile and entrap and lead to ruin the souls of men. "Who," he cried from his throne, "will go to earth and persuade men to accomplish the ruin of their soul?" "I will go," answered one of the dark spirits as he came forward. "And what will you say to them?" "I will persuade them that there is no God." "No," said the king of hell, "that will not do. You can never persuade the majority of men that there is no God. They may say that, but in their heart they will not believe it. Created by God, man will always believe that there is a God, for the voice of God speaks in his nature." Then a second dark spirit glided forward and said, "I will go." "And what wilt thou do?" said the king of hell. "I will persuade them that there is no heaven." "No," said the king of lost spirits, "that will not do. Men expect a future life. The instincts of their heart tell them of a land of happiness and bliss, that land from which you and I, infernal spirits, have fallen." Then came forward a third demon and said, "I will go." "What wilt thou say?" said the king of hell. "I will persuade men that there is no hell." "No," said Satan, "that will not do. You cannot persuade men that there is no hell. There are too many pangs of conscience here to believe that. We must have something else, something that will appeal to all men in all conditions, of all ages, of all beliefs."

Then a fourth dark spirit glided forward and whispered to Satan, "I will go." "And what wilt thou tell them?" said Satan. "I will tell them there is no hurry." "Tomorrow!"

ABRAHAM—A PIONEER'S EPITAPH

XIV

"Into the land of Canaan they came"

Genesis 12: 5

HERE is the epitaph on the graves of those brave pioneers who followed Abraham from far-off Ur of the Chaldees to the land of Canaan in the most memorable of all emigrations. "They went forth to go into the land of Canaan; and into the land of Canaan they came." They started for Canaan, and they kept going till they reached it.

A number of years ago I picked up in London a two-penny pamphlet biography of Joseph Chamberlain, the famous English statesman. It told how he had been in his youth a Sunday school teacher at Birmingham, and how his favorite verse in the Bible was this verse from the twelfth chapter of Genesis, "They went forth into the land of Canaan; and into the land of Canaan they came." It was a verse well suited to a man of his ambition, iron will, determination, and perseverance.

There are two qualifications for success in life. One is to have a goal for which we start—they went forth to go into the land of Canaan. The second is to keep on going after we have started—"Into the land of Canaan they came."

Abraham was the father of all who take to the highway. The land for which he started was Canaan. The account in Genesis would seem to make the call of God come to Abraham in Haran, where he stopped for a time on his westward journey; whereas Stephen's speech in the book of Acts makes the call come to Abraham in Ur of the Chaldees. The reconciliation is probably to be found in the fact that he was called first in Ur of Chaldees, and a second time in Haran. God said to him, "Get thee out of thy country, and from thy kindred, and from thy father's house, unto a land that I will show thee." Abraham obeyed the call, and went forth to go into the land of Canaan. This was not done without great difficulties. As God said in his call to Abraham, he had to forsake his country and his kindred. That is not easy, even today. I remember once at the harbor at Queenstown leaning over the rail of the Lusitania, soon to be sunk in those very waters, and watching the farewells of the Irish immigrants on the deck of the tender below. They had been stirred by ambition to start out for their land of Canaan, America; but now the thought that they were seeing for the last time the green hills of Ireland, and the faces of their friends, filled them with woe. Abraham forsook his country and his people and started for the west.

When he had gone about halfway to the land of Haran, he rested there for a time, and there his old father, Terah, died. "The days of Terah were two hundred and five years: and Terah died in Haran." The comforts and the ease of Haran, with its pastures and its plentiful waters, must have appealed strongly to Abraham; but in addition to all this there was now the sepulcher of his father. The ancient peoples were strongly attached to the graves of their kindred. Stopping one night at a mountain cabin in Kentucky, I talked with the aged man and his wife about their life in their narrow and rugged valley. They told me that many years before they had started to migrate westward to the fertile bluegrass region of Kentucky. But they had gone only a few days' journey when they turned back to their mountain home, "because," said this old withered woman, "we didn't want to be so far away from the graves of our kin." Abraham forsook the grave of his father and went forth to go into the land of Canaan.

He encountered all kinds of difficulties and dangers—drought, lurking bands of robbers, sandstorms, plagues, sickness, and fatigue. But he kept on, true to the start he had made; and at length at the end of his long trek he came up out of the

Jordan and trod the land of Canaan. "They went forth to go into the land of Canaan; and into the land of Canaan they came."

I. The Destination and the Goal

Where are you going? With many the answer would be, "Just going." They never get anywhere, because they never start for any place. A drunken man one day lurched up to the ticket window in a railroad station and asked for a ticket. To the impatient inquiry of the ticket seller, "Where to?" the man responded, "What tickets have you?" No one gets out of the road of a man who is just sauntering idly along the sidewalk; but when you see a man come sweeping along with vigorous stride, you make way for him.

The want of a purpose and a worth-while objective in life leaves a character unstable, weak, and an attractive target for the temptations of life. Asked about certain temptations and follies, Edison replied that he had never felt their power because he had been so engrossed in his scientific experiments. "The great misfortune of my life," wrote Robert Burns, "was to want an aim." To this lack of aim in life he attributed his lapse from innocence and the dissipations into which he fell. An honorable ambition is a strong anchor to hold one steady amid the storms and tides of temptation and sin.

II. Why Some Who Start for the Land of Canaan Never Reach It

First, there are those who start and then go back. The hardships and the difficulties of the way frighten them from their goal. The Jews were all enthusiasm when they started on the Exodus from Egypt for the land of Canaan. But erelong we find them murmuring and complaining of their difficulties and dangers and hankering after the fleshpots of Egypt. Frightened by the report of the giants in the land, they were turned back to wander for forty years, until all the generation that had murmured were dead. In *Pilgrim's Progress,* Christian, just starting from the City of Destruction for the Celestial City, on his way up the Hill Difficulty met two men, Timorous and Mistrust, running in opposite directions. They told him that they, too, had set out for the City of Zion, but that just a little further along there were a couple of lions lying in the path. Many start for Canaan, but not all arrive. Lions in the path turn them back.

Another reason why some who start never arrive is that they are tempted to try other goals and start off in other directions. If Abraham had experimented with other lands and other directions, he never would have arrived in Canaan. Suppose that someone had met him on the highroad to the West, telling him that there were reports of a much finer country lying to the South; and then that on the road to that south country he had met someone else with glowing reports of a prosperous country lying to the North, and started on that trail. Never would this great verse have been written about him, "To the land of Canaan he came." Writing about his course and his goal, and likening himself to a racer in the Corinthian games, Paul said that he ran "not as uncertainly." It is a striking picture of incompetence and inefficiency, that of a runner on the course, not certain of the direction in which he wants to run. Yet, on life's race course there are not a few such runners. The apostle said, "This one thing I do."

Lincoln used to tell the story of a man who heated a piece of iron in the forge, not knowing just what he was going to make out of it. At first he thought he would make a horseshoe; then he changed his mind and thought he would make something else out of it. After he had hammered on this plan for a little while, he changed his mind and started on something else. By this time, he had so hammered the iron that it was not good for much of anything, and holding it up with his tongs, the blacksmith looked at it in disgust, and thrusting it hissing into a tub of water, exclaimed, "Well, at least, I can make a fizzle out of it." It is better to concentrate on one thing than to dream about a hundred things. How often in old age is heard the echo of this sigh coming from the lips of men who have made no mark for themselves, "If I had only followed one thing!"

Others never reach Canaan because they settle down in the halfway country of Haran. In Haran there are green oases, palm trees, lush pastures, running waters, immunity from dust and heat and hostile tribesmen. Every now and then you come across somebody who has settled down in Haran. He started out to be something, but never arrived. He gave up his dreams and ambitions and took out naturalization papers as a citizen of Haran.

III. The Triumph at the End

"Into the land of Canaan they came!" What a ring that has to it! I can imagine Abraham's emotion as he came up out of the swelling Jordan and viewed the landscape o'er. There was the Canaan of his dreams. That was the goal he had seen away down in Mesopotamia. By faith and by perseverance he had reached the end of the journey. The Scotch used to have a prayer that they might be granted an "honorable through-bearing." It is not enough to start with enthusiasm; we must go through to the end.

Coming into New York from New Jersey, in the days before the tubes were built, it was a source of never-ending delight to me to stand on the upper deck of the ferryboat and watch the craft of all description going up the North River to their docks. There go the ships; ships from all parts of the world. There was the stately bark or brigantine laden with silks, or teas, or spices, that had slipped down some river in Siam or China, had sailed through the typhoon-infested China Sea, skirted the coral islands of the South Pacific, turned the stormy and dangerous Horn, then through the South Atlantic and the tempestuous North Atlantic to New York, and now was being towed by a tug to her berth in Hoboken or Staten Island. There was the one-funneled fruiter that came from Panama and Colon and Havana, and whose twelve manner of fruits would in a day or two be sold on the streets of New York, Boston, Philadelphia, Pittsburgh, and Chicago. And there was the private yacht, trim and white; and yonder the tramp steamer laden with the merchandise of Britain or Germany; and here the low-lying battleship with its military masts and its signals flying, and its naked guns peering out with wicked eye; and passing on this side, the great four-decked liner from Liverpool or Hamburg or Havre, its sirens sounding a hoarse warning, and bearing its cargo of thousands of human lives, some coming home again, others from the steppes of Russia, or the Mediterranean lands, and looking with hope and wonder on the far-famed city of the New World, with its towers of Babel reaching heavenward. There go the ships! Through mist and fog and snow and rain and calm and gale; through seas that were chill with icebergs, and others that were as blue as heaven's vault. From Europe, South America, Asia, the West Indies, the

Pacific Coast, these ships had come; and as they move up the river they seem to say to the world that was waiting for them, "I have finished the course!"

This is a double truth with which I have been dealing. On the surface, we have thought of the honorable ambitions and dreams for this life; but underneath there has been always the thought of that highest goal of all—Christian character and the salvation of the soul. You may not be sure whether you are fitted to be a doctor, lawyer, artist, musician, or business man. But you can be certain of this: you are called of God to the land of faith and Christian character. Just as certainly as God called Abraham out of Mesopotamia, so he calls you. "Arise," God says, "get thee out!"

The way is long and hard. You must make denials and renunciations. Fierce temptations will assail you. Pleasant and comfortable Harans with sweet-murmuring fountains and grateful shade and dark-eyed companions will do all they can do to allure and detain you. Where are you going? And if that is where you want to go, are you on the right road now? And do you know how far you are from the goal? Some here today, no doubt, must be numbered among those who have started and have gone back. It is a word that has dropped out of religious phraseology, but it is a good scriptural word, and will suit the case of some here today as no other word will. That word is "backslider." You started and have gone back. But the land to which you have returned will never satisfy you. Your true country is that for which you started. Others here have stopped halfway, and have dropped into the easy life of the halfway country. Now is the time to strike the tents and start again for Canaan. Others are here who started and have been diverted from their true course, turned aside into weird and dangerous byways of loose religious ideas, and getting further and further from the highway of salvation. They are like the man whose epitaph our Lord wrote: "This man began to build, but could not finish."

And some perhaps have never started. But the sun is high. Soon it will be midday, and then the afternoon, and after that the night, when no man can travel. Thinking, planning, talking, studying the road map is not enough. The one thing to do is to start. Arise, and go forth to go unto the land of Canaan! You will find many all around you who have turned back, and a great many others who might be described as "halfwayers." But these are not the ones whom you ought to take for your guides. Be led and inspired, rather, by those who started and who have arrived at their goal; those who said, "This one thing I do"; those who lived to say too, "I have finished the course"; those on whose grave is written this thrilling epitaph, "They went forth to go into the land of Cannan; and into the land of Canaan they came."

SOLOMON'S WIVES

XV

"His wives turned away his heart after other gods"

I Kings 11: 4

WE do not know where Solomon's numerous wives are buried; but here is the grave of Solomon, and here is the epitaph on the grave of the greatest and wisest of kings, "His wives turned away his heart after other gods."

An Italian artist painted a picture of Solomon in the Day of Resurrection. Solomon is looking doubtfully upon two processions of souls, some on the way to Life Eternal, some to darkness and condemnation. He is not sure to which group he belongs. Thus the artist has put into painting the doubt in men's minds as to the final state and fate of Solomon, whether we are to number him among the redeemed souls, or think of him as finally apostate and rejected of God. Nothing could have been brighter than Solomon's morning; nothing more glorious than his noonday; nothing darker and gloomier than his evening.

Solomon is at once the best known and the least known of Bible characters. His very name is a synonym for wealth, wisdom, splendor, and fame. Centuries after his reign Christ could refer to "Solomon in all his glory" as the perfection of human splendor and glory. Yet at the same time, Solomon is one of the least known of the characters of the Bible. You see the glitter of his riches and behold him exalted upon his throne and listen to his Songs and Proverbs; but Solomon the man you never come to know, as you do David his father, or Peter in the New Testament. Something very grand and splendid about Solomon; and yet something which suggests an immense and melancholy shadow. Solomon was the child of real love, the son of Bathsheba, who played such a tragic part in the drama of King David's life. Perhaps children of such union are more gifted than others. Solomon certainly was one of the most gifted of men, and his beautiful and ambitious mother used her influence with David when that king lay on his deathbed to secure his elevation to the throne.

I. Solomon's Choice

The beginning of Solomon's reign was full of promise for the future. A great celebration took place at the time of his inauguration at Gibeon where the tabernacle was, when thousands of animals were sacrificed and the people gave thanks to God. That same night Solomon had a marvelous dream. In the dream God appeared to Solomon and said to him, "Ask what I shall give thee." There was no reservation and no suggestion as to what he should ask. It was solemnly left to the young king to make his choice for himself. That is true of us all. What did Solomon ask? This was his request: "Give me wisdom and knowledge, that I may go out and come in before this people. Give thy servant an understanding heart, that I may discern between good and bad." This was Solomon's memorable choice; and because he had not asked riches, nor long life, nor vengeance upon his enemies, as most kings would have asked, God not only granted his request, but told him that riches and power and long life would be added to the gift of wisdom. When the young Queen Victoria was awakened on the night of June 20, 1837, after the death of William IV, Lord Melbourne, after notifying her that she was now Queen of England, opened the Bible and read to her this account of Solomon's dream and Solomon's choice.

But the story of Solomon's dream is one which applies not only to kings and queens, but to all men, for we are all kings and princes in the sight of God. Suppose that God appeared to you in a dream tonight and said, "Ask what thou wilt," what would be your request? One has said that if all our wishes were gratified our pleasures would be destroyed. I suppose that that means that men wish for wrong or foolish things, and also, that if all their desires were gratified they would not have the pleasure of wishing. You have heard of wishing wells and wishing stairs. On the old wall at Chester there is a stairway which is known as the wishing steps. Imagine that such a place has real, and not fancied, power to grant your wish, for what would you ask? The question is not so simple as it seems. Discontented though most people are, if placed on the wishing steps, or if spoken to in a dream, like Solomon, and invited to ask what they will have, they would be hard put to make the choice.

In a sense, we all dream Solomon's dream. In the higher meaning of life we all have opportunity to choose and have what we will. "Ask what I shall give thee!" Some would ask for money. It is evident from the struggles and the speech of many persons that that is their chief desire. An American millionaire, leaving the other day for Europe, gave this advice to young men, "Do not struggle for riches. I have struggled for them and secured them, and there is not much to it." Others would choose power, or fame, or beauty, or affection, or the silencing of an accusing conscience which follows them day and night and says unto them, "Thou art the man." Only a few would ask for wisdom, for the understanding heart, for a clear knowledge of good and evil, and the will to do the good. That was what

Solomon asked for. It was an unusual request for a king, in that or in any age. We all have a choice, and in our dreams at least we can do well. Solomon did not ask for a long life, but for a good life.

"We live in deeds, not years; in thoughts, not breaths;
In feelings, not in figures on a dial.
We should count time by heart-throbs. He most lives
Who thinks most, feels the noblest, acts the best." [1]

II. The Splendor and Fame of Solomon

Solomon's reputation for wisdom was soon put to the test. His fame had traveled all over the earth, and from as far off as Ethiopia the Queen of Sheba came to try him with her questions. Her conclusion was that the half had never yet been told. How true that is of the wisdom and love of a greater than Solomon! When one really comes to know and love Christ, that experience and satisfaction go beyond anything that he has been told concerning it, whether by prophet, or apostle. How true that is also concerning the goodness of God in the life to come. The half has never yet been told. Could the inhabitants of the world of redeemed spirits speak to you and me, I am sure that is what they would say, "The half has never yet been told." "Eye hath not seen, ear hath not heard, neither have entered into the mind of man the things which God hath prepared for them that love him."

[1] Philip James Bailey.

The other well-known instance of the wisdom of Solomon was the story of the two harlots who slept together with their newly born babes in the same bed. The one mother overlaid her child and it died. With mother love, and yet with wicked cunning, she arose in the night and took the living babe out of its mother's arms and laid the dead babe where the living child had been. In the morning the mother of the living child discovered the substitution and demanded back her babe. The woman refused, and the extraordinary case was brought before the king. Solomon solved the problem in a way that showed his knowledge of the human heart, for he called for a sword and commanded that the living child be cut in two, one-half given to the one mother and one-half to the other. The lying mother assented to this, but the true mother cried out, "O my lord, give her the living child and in no wise slay it." This event made Solomon as famous as any in his long reign. There have been stories similar to it; for example, the story of Ariphanes of Thrace and the three young men who claimed to be sons of the deceased king of the Cimmerians. Ariphanes ordered that each one hurl a javelin at the father's corpse. Two of the young men at once obeyed. The third refused to do so, and him Ariphanes declared to be the true son and the successor to his father.

Solomon ransacked the world for riches and trophies. Horses and chariots by the thousands he brought up from Egypt. His navies plowed the most distant seas and brought apes, ivory, and peacocks from far-off lands. He gathered "gold as tin," as Ecclesiasticus puts it, and "multiplied silver as lead."

Solomon was a great builder, too. There is a tradition that he built palaces in far-off Palmyra and temples at Baalbek. His own palace took thirteen years in the building. Nor was he unmindful of the defenses of his kingdom. At his direction great fortifications were built at Millo and elsewhere by his engineers. He made alliance with the kings and rulers of the powerful states of the world at that time. In the intellectual realm, also, his achievements were great. "He spake three thousand proverbs: and his songs were a thousand and five." He was at once the Augustus and the Aristotle of his kingdom and of his age. "He spake of trees, from the cedar tree that is in Lebanon even unto the hyssop that springeth out of the wall: he spake also of beasts, and of fowl, and of creeping things, and of fishes."

As a builder Solomon's great achievement was the temple of Jehovah at Jerusalem. This was the solemn trust that had been laid upon him by his father. Because David had been a man of blood, of so many fierce wars, he was not permitted to build the temple which was to be a house of peace. That distinction fell to Solomon and nobly did he fulfill his task. The temple of Solomon has long since crumbled into dust.

Fire, sword, sack and battle, wind and weather, have long ago destroyed the temple that Solomon built. Perhaps a few stones of it are left on that rock that is now Jerusalem, but even that is conjectural. But the prayer, one of the sublimest that ever fell from the lips of man, that Solomon offered at the dedication of the temple remains to this day, not a stone of its faith missing, not a pinnacle of its aspiration broken, not an altar of its confession and supplication overturned. Temples made with hands disappear; but the temple of thought, of aspiration, of worship, of adoration, of faith—that is indestructible. It remains in all its beauty and grandeur from generation to generation.

III. Solomon's Fall

How terrible that such a man should fall into an abyss so deep as did Solomon! The man who when he came to the throne had asked the understanding heart, to know the difference between the good and the bad, who had filled the earth with the fame of his wisdom and his splendor; and yet here is his epitaph, "His wives turned away his heart."

The last chapter of Solomon's life makes sad reading. He had outlived his reputation and his popularity. His ambition for great buildings that should vie with the colossal structures of Egypt and of Tyre, led him to oppress his people, and thousands of Hebrews were compelled to labor on these structures.

These exactions and the heavy taxes which fell upon the people destroyed the popularity of Solomon. The relationship which he established with outside kingdoms made him compromise with idolatry. Step by step, Solomon turned away from the God he had chosen in his youth and who had blessed him and prospered him as no other king. Then we read that God, who had appeared twice unto Solomon, both times to bless him, now appeared unto him with words of judgment. Adversaries were raised up against him—Hadad, Rezon, and Jeroboam; and the last we hear of the apostate, lonely, and unhappy king is that he sought to lay a murderer's hand upon Jeroboam. Then came death, and a night so dark that, as Frederick Robertson has said in his fine sermon on Solomon, we do not know whether it will have a dawn or not. Both the Kings and the Chronicles dismiss Solomon with the bare record of his death, "Solomon slept with his fathers." That is all they have to say of him at the end of his reign of forty years of power and splendor; not a word of praise, not a word of admiration. Evidently the kingdom was not sorry when it heard that Solomon was dead. "He departed without being desired."

When one reviews the character of Solomon, it is impossible not to think of another fall, the fall of another of the wisest men of history, Francis Bacon, of whom his biographer said, "He rose to the highest place and honor, and yet that place and honor were but the fringe and adornment of all that made him great. It is difficult to imagine a grander and more magnificent career; and his name ranks among the few chosen examples of human achievement; and yet it was not only an unhappy life, it was a poor life. We expect that such an overwhelming weight of glory should be borne up by a character corresponding to it in strength and nobleness. But that is not what we find. No one ever had a greater idea of what he was made for. . . . But he was not true to what he knew. He cringed to such a man as Buckingham. He sold himself to the corrupt and ignominious government of James I. He was willing to be employed to hunt to death a friend like Essex. . . . To Bacon the most loving and generous of benefactors."

Bacon wrote the wonderful essays on Death, and Truth, and Adversity. Some are sure that he wrote the plays which bear the name of Shakespeare. He touched nothing that he did not adorn. Yet he fell like Lucifer, and not without reason has been called "the wisest, brightest, meanest of mankind." So when we think of Solomon we may well call him the wisest man and the greatest fool in the history of mankind.

When Daniel Webster delivered his celebrated 7th of March Speech in the United States Senate, 1850, which to many of his friends seemed a bid for the Presidency at the cost of compromise with the Fugitive Slave Law and with slavery, Whittier wrote his poem, "Ichabod." Whether what he said of Webster was true or not, it is true of Solomon.

"So fallen! so lost! the light withdrawn
Which once he wore!
The glory from his gray hairs gone
Forevermore!

Revile him not; the Tempter hath
A snare for all;
And pitying tears, not scorn and wrath,
Befit his fall!

Oh, dumb be passion's stormy rage,
When he who might
Have lighted up and led his age,
Falls back in night.

Scorn! would the angels laugh, to mark
A bright soul driven,
Fiend-goaded, down the endless dark,
From hope and heaven!"

What was the cause of Solomon's apostasy and fall? What was it that brought on this black and terrible night to Solomon's life? No doubt, worldly ambition and pride played their part. Solomon had established friendly relations with the great kingdoms of his day. He wanted to vie with them in splendor, in wealth, and in great buildings. This must have had an evil effect upon his own religious life. Too much of the world, too much prosperity, too much power, too much engrossment in the things of the world have a tendency to separate the heart from righteousness and from God. It was certainly so in Solomon's case.

But the Bible makes no mystery of the fall of Solomon. In the plainest of words it tells us that he loved many strange women, and that these wives with whom he crowded his vast harem at Jerusalem "turned away his heart after other gods." For these wives, brought from Egypt and Moab, from the Ammonites and the Edomites, and from the Zidonians and the Hittites, Solomon built altars to the heathen gods, and within sight of the very temple of God there was a high place, where with unclean and licentious rites sacrifices were made to the heathen gods.

There is Solomon for you; the young king who asked for the understanding heart, who sang a thousand songs, and spoke three thousand proverbs, and prayed the most beautiful prayer of which we have any record: but now a sensual and licentious Sybarite, surrounded by a host of foreign women who bend him to their will. What could be more dismal, more astounding, more melancholy than the fall of Solomon, and what more terrible than the cause of it?

The author of the great book, the Apocryphal book of Ecclesiasticus, sums up the story of Solomon's fall in these words: "Thou didst bow thy loins unto women, *and by thy body thou wast brought into subjection.*" True and memorable saying, that is.

Alas, how many good and wise, inspired and noble in one way or another, win that epitaph for themselves, "By thy body thou wast brought into subjection."

David had warned Solomon that God "would not fail him nor forsake him, if he sought him with his whole heart; but that if he forsook God, he would cast him off forever." The fall of Solomon raises that question. Was he cast off forever? On the side of the hope of a final restoration, for this king who was once so wise and so good, and whose reign is a type of the reign of Christ, there is, first of all, the prophecy made by the good prophet Nathan, to David before the birth of Solomon, that this son would build a house for the glory of God; and that if he committed iniquity God would punish him with the rod of men. Then comes this sentence, "But my mercy shall not depart from him."

Then we have the comment of Nehemiah, who protested in his day against the marriage of the Jews with foreign women, and yet remembered that even Solomon had been guilty of this sin. "Nevertheless, even him did outlandish women cause to sin." But he also says, "Among many nations there was no king like him who was beloved of his God." Some take that to mean that Nehemiah held that Solomon, in spite of his terrible fall, was still beloved of God and accepted by him. It is hard to think that a man who could make the choice that Solomon did in his early life, and who could utter a prayer like that at the dedication of the temple, will be finally lost. As to his punishments and sufferings, there can be no doubt. If Solomon is not the author of the Book of Ecclesiastes, certainly he is the personality and king into whose mouth the author puts the melancholy sentiments of that book. "Vanity of vanity!" that was all Solomon got out of his great experience with the world and its splendor. The only reality is God, and let us not forget that that is the conclusion of the book of Ecclesiastes—"Fear God, and keep his commandments."

"This world is all a fleeting show,
For man's illusion given;
The smiles of joy, the tears of woe,
Deceitful shine, deceitful flow—
There's nothing true but Heaven." [2]

Thus the career of Solomon points the way to everything good and true in life. If men choose, as he chose, and are faithful to their choice, as he was not, life brings great joys and great rewards. But his fall tells us that the wisest and greatest of men, the most gifted of personalities, can plunge into the deepest and most terrible of sins, and that the whole substance and beauty of life can be reduced to dust and ashes and summed up in that mournful phrase, "Vanity of vanities."

[2] Thomas Moore.

I like to think that Nathan's prediction gives us the final word about Solomon; that, although God punished him for his sins, he did not take his mercy from him, and that mercy, the mercy which has been made known to mankind by a greater than Solomon, brought Solomon back to the favor of God. I like to think that Solomon not only said it in his sublime prayer at the dedication of the temple, but found what he said to be true: "If they sin against thee, for there is no man that sinneth not, and thou be angry with them, and deliver them to the enemy; so that they carry them away captives unto the land of the enemy; yet if they shall bethink themselves, and repent, and make supplication unto thee, saying, We have sinned; and so return unto thee with all their heart, and with all their soul: then hear thou their prayer and their supplication in heaven." I like to think that the history that Solomon sketched there of a man's sin and disobedience and forgiveness was fulfilled in his own life, and that as a penitent sinner he came back to God.

How wonderful that promise is, "My mercy shall not depart away from him." Let every wandering soul remember that! Let everyone who has turned away from the pious dreams of his youth, everyone who has been led into transgression or sin—yes, let all of us, for, as Solomon said, "Who is there that sinneth not?"—let all of us remember that God has said, He will not take his mercy away from us. Let us seek now the mercy of God in Christ.

There is the sad epitaph on the grave of the wisest and greatest of kings: "His wives turned away his heart." But underneath it, when you push back the grass and the weeds, you can see another inscription, a second epitaph. It is this: and let us never forget it, for we shall all need it—"My mercy shall not depart away from him."

GOD'S SOCIAL REGISTER

XVI

"Jabez was more honorable than his brethren"

I Chronicles 4: 9

TABLES of genealogy make dull reading. When we come to them in the Bible we generally skip them and go on to something more interesting. Yet they have their place in the inspired Scriptures, and it is worth while to read through these dreary catalogues of names, for here and there, just as one finds a flower growing amid the ruins of Ephesus or Antioch, you come upon the record of some noble and useful life. Here is such a record. In the list of these names of men who were born, begat, and died, and are dismissed by the Chronicler, you find this exquisite and fragrant flower of biography blooming amid the ruins and relics of the past. "Jabez was more honorable than his brethren." In this graveyard of the dead here is one man of whom something more is said than merely that he was born, lived, and died. He receives honorable mention for the qualities of the soul.

Most cities have what they call a Social Register; sometimes a Blue Book, or a Red Book, wherein are inscribed the names of those who move in what is called "society." But God has his own Blue Book, where are entered the names of those who have achieved beauty of character. That is the only true distinction. Imagine, if you can, an angel of heaven asking one of the redeemed spirits about the family, the social station in this world, of another and recently arrived redeemed spirit! How absurd, how unthinkable, for there the only distinction is the distinction of the soul.

> "There is
> One great society alone on earth:
> The noble living and the noble dead." [1]

Let us look more closely at this thumbnail biography of Jabez which we find here in the midst of this table of ancient genealogy.

I. Heredity

When you come upon the record of a remarkable life like this, distinguished for qualities of the soul, you can be certain that back of this man there is a line of worthy and godly ancestry. In the case of Jabez we are able to trace this line. He came of the Kenites, and was therefore a descendant of the

[1] Wordsworth, "The Prelude."

Rechabites, whose chief Jonadab, in order to preserve their simplicity of manners and their morals, commanded them to dwell in tents and to abstain from wine and all intoxicating liquor. Ages after, Jeremiah found these people still faithful to their vows, and the promise was given them that they should not want a man to stand before God forever.

When God chose a man to do some particular ministry, not infrequently he was set apart from the ordinary customs of life by the vow of the Nazarite, which included total abstinence from strong drink. This was true of Samson, and of a far greater than Samson, John the Baptist. Thus we see that Jabez came of a godly, self-denying line of people, among whom there was plain living and high thinking. Men do not gather grapes of thorns, nor figs of thistles. Whence came John Milton with his glorious vision and gift of song? And whence came Oliver Cromwell with his shaking down of that which was unjust and evil? Whence, but from the Puritans, the Rechabites of that age?

The only heredity about which one is justified in boasting is the heredity of a godly ancestry. In the beautiful lines, "On the Receipt of My Mother's Picture," William Cowper says:

> "My boast is not, that I deduce my birth
> From loins enthroned and rulers of the earth;
> But higher far my proud pretentions rise—
> The son of parents passed into the skies!"

II. Overcoming Handicaps

His mother named her child Jabez, which means "he makes sorrow." "His mother called his name Jabez, saying, Because I bare him with sorrow." We wonder what lies back of that record. Did it mean that he was a posthumous child, that his father was dead? Did it mean that this mother foresaw the long, grim struggle with poverty that awaited her and him? Or did it mean that he was an unwanted child? Whatever it was, Jabez entered upon life under some kind of a handicap. What mysteries there are in life and character! Children who come into the world with the best start, and are surrounded with every advantage, stimulated with every possible training, will amount to nothing; whereas children who are flung out, as it were, into the midst of the world, with everything against them, and with apparently no chance at all, rise to usefulness and eminence and become more honorable than their brethren.

Early in the last century, the Presbyterian minister at Darlington, Pennsylvania, out on his pastoral round, was riding his horse down a country lane. As he drew up before a humble cottage, he heard the sound of a woman's voice lifted in earnest prayer. As he listened he heard this widowed mother, with her boys kneeling at her side, earnestly entreating God that he would open a door for the education of these boys, so that they might become good and useful men. The pastor dismounted and went in to speak with the widow who had prayed so earnestly, and yet with a note of sorrow in her voice. Struck with the alertness of one of these boys, and touched by the woman's petitions, he took the boy with him to the old Stone Academy at Darlington, and there gave him the instruction for which his mother had prayed. That boy, so handicapped in his birth, and for whom there seemed to be no opportunity, influenced more young minds in America in the last century than any other man, for it was William McGuffey, the author of the famous Eclectic Readers, which reached the extraordinary circulation of 2,000,000 copies.

The Presbyterian Church celebrates this year the centennial of the achievements in Oregon of the missionaries, Henry Harman Spalding and Marcus Whitman, two of the noblest heroes in the long roll call of Presbyterian missionaries. This Henry Harman Spalding was an exception to the general law of heredity, in that he came into the world an illegitimate and unwanted child. Even the foster mother, who took him in, cast him out when he was a lad, and the boy, a stranger to all the ordinary joys of boyhood, wished that he might die. Yet he overcame the handicaps of his birth and early life and lived to write one of the most heroic pages of the modern Acts of the Apostles of Christ.

III. Jabez Was a Man of Prayer

The others who are mentioned here were begotten, begat others in turn, and then died. That is all that is said of them. But it is written of Jabez, who was more honorable than his brethren, that "he called on the God of Israel." Of the others nothing is said, save their birth and their death. But Jabez was a man of prayer. That, evidently, was the secret of the nobility of his life, and the reason for the immortality of his fame. The Holy Spirit, who delights to linger over the name of Jabez, has preserved for us the remarkable prayer which he made.

The first thing that strikes one about that prayer is its deep earnestness and urgency of petition, "O that thou wouldst bless me indeed." Jabez held that God was the source of every blessing, and that without his favor life could not be truly blessed. He asked that God would bless him *indeed.* There are blessings that shine brightly and appear to be blessings, but are not so "indeed." On the other hand, what may seem at the time anything but a blessing—adversities, hardship, pain, sorrow—may in the end prove to be a blessing "indeed." Jabez wants a real blessing, in whatever form God chooses to send it. He wants the blessing that maketh rich and addeth no sorrow therewith. Once I listened to a remarkable farewell address given by a venerable college president to the graduating class on Commencement Day. He told them that he hoped that they would have a degree of success in life, and in their chosen callings and professions; but that his chief desire for them, and that of the college they were leaving, was that they might be men and women of God. There was a college president who prayed for his young men and young women that they might be blessed "indeed."

Jabez asked for temporal things. "O that thou wouldst enlarge my coast." We are encouraged, and in the Lord's Prayer we have the example of Christ, to pray for temporal blessings. Some people who scoff at the idea of asking God for temporal blessings, as if that were unworthy of a true believer, know better than some of the great wrestlers with God, such as Jacob, and Jabez, who asked God to enlarge his coast, and Christ, who in our Lord's Prayer taught us to say, "Give us this day our daily bread." In that great prayer spiritual and temporal good are joined together. It is right that we should ask God to bless us in "our basket and in our store."

But that phrase, "Enlarge my coast," opens a door to higher things than even the necessary good of this world. It makes us think of the larger and more abundant life, of wider sympathies, of increasing knowledge, and of deepening faith and love. What a great many people need to lift them out of their littleness, and sometimes out of their meanness and wickedness, is the enlarged coast, to see and believe and possess the greater things, and the life which is more than meat, and the body which is more than raiment.

Jabez prayed also for divine guidance. "O that thine hand might be with me." The Bible makes beautiful use of the hand of God. What you have here is a picture of God's hand on a man's shoulder, or taking the pilgrim by the hand and leading him in the way. Jabez wants the hand of God to be with him. Whichever way he turns, and in whatever he undertakes, he will do it only after asking God's guidance and seeking God's permission. We all come to times and places when we are not sure which way to turn; and yet we seem to realize that much depends, as to our future welfare and happiness, upon the decision we make or the way in which we turn. Always, at least, before we make the decision, or take one road instead of another, we can ask that God will bless the decision. Then, no matter what comes, we can be sure that there is some good and some blessing in it for us. "In all thy ways acknowledge him, and he will direct thy paths."

"Through each perplexing path of life,
Our wandering footsteps guide,
Give us each day our daily bread,
And raiment fit provide."

The last and greatest petition of Jabez was this: "O that thou wouldest keep me from evil, that it may not grieve me!" Jabez had the true philosophy of life. The one thing from which we ought to pray to be kept is evil. The one root sorrow, the one fountainhead of woe and suffering in life, is moral evil. Nothing grieves like that. There is no sadness like the sadness of sin, there is no night like the darkness of evil. There are men and women all about us today who carry with them some kind of grief or sorrow or pain or trouble. It may be a thorn in the flesh; it may be a disappointment of the heart; it may be a concern for a loved one; it may be a deep anxiety for the morrow. It may be a concern about the very necessities of life; it may be the sharp wound of unkindness or ingratitude or slander or injustice. But all these are as nothing compared with the grief and pain that come to man through sin, through the evil that is in the world. Christ taught us to repeat the prayer of Jabez when he told us to pray, "Lead us not into temptation, but deliver us from evil." And in his own great prayer on the night on which he was betrayed, when he prayed for his disciples, and for all those who in ages to come should through them believe on his name, he said, "I pray not that thou shouldst take them out of the world, but that thou shouldst keep them from the evil."

Such, then, was the prayer of Jabez. How beautiful and fragrant still is this flower which we have found amid the dusty ruins and broken stones of a forgotten world. It is a prayer that all of us would do well to make, when every day we begin a new life and go forth into the world. The world has changed greatly in outward form since Jabez lived and died. But man has not changed; sin has not changed. It has lost nothing of its power to grieve, to wound, and to hurt. Still, with all our vaunted knowledge, we know so little of ourselves, of the world about us, and of the tomorrow. Therefore, we can all pray that God would bless us indeed, enlarge the coasts of our life, guide us with his hand, and keep us from the evil that is in the world.

The name of Jabez is forever enrolled in the Social Register of God. He was more honorable than his brethren. Strive for that distinction! Rejoice not in the passing things of this world which entertain and please for but a moment and then are gone, but rejoice rather that your names are written in Heaven, in the Lamb's Book of Life.

JESUS—THE EPITAPH THAT ENDS ALL EPITAPHS

XVII

"He is not here: for he is risen"

Matthew 28: 6

MOST epitaphs are written by man concerning man. They give a true or false estimate of the character of the dead, and express, or fail to express, hope for the future. But here is an epitaph written, or spoken, not by man, but by an angel. This epitaph is not a eulogy, nor an estimate of character, nor the expression of a pious wish or hope; but just a bare fact, and yet the most momentous of all facts. "He is not here: for he is risen!"

The handling of spirits in a narrative is said to be the highest test of genius. If so, the Gospel narratives certainly stand the test, for what could be more fitting, more beautiful, more calm and natural, than the words and the actions of the angels who appeared at the tomb. The two Marys had gone out early in the morning to the sepulcher. There they met the angels. Matthew and Mark say one angel, or a young man; Luke and John, two angels. These angels make to them the announcement that the grave is empty and that Christ is risen. They announced the fact of the empty grave, which was a supernatural fact; and since such a fact had to be interpreted, they gave the interpretation and explanation of it. "He is risen."

Most epitaphs, no matter how beautifully worded, proclaim the power of death; but here is an epitaph which tells that the power of death is forever broken. This is the epitaph which ends all epitaphs. It will put an end to death, for it will put an end to that which brought death in the world, sin. As we stand by the side of the two Marys in the garden and hear again the pronouncement of the angels, "He is not here: for he is risen," let us look, first, at the Fact of the Resurrection, and then at the Meaning of the Fact.

I. The Fact of the Resurrection

There is no Easter message or Easter hope without the Easter fact. Christianity consists of great hopes, precepts, joys; but it stands upon three great facts—the Incarnation, the Crucifixion, and the Resurrection.

The first heralds of the Resurrection were these women who went early to the tomb. They reached the conclusion that the grave was empty and that Christ was risen in two ways. First of all, by the announcement of the angels. The angels make the same announcement to us through the Scriptures as they did to these women. The long history of the Christian Church in the world, this Easter service today, and every church spire, every church bell, repeats and echoes the proclamation of the angels, "He is not here: for he is risen."

This is the greatest announcement that the world has ever heard, greater even than that which the angels spoke to the shepherds at Bethlehem when Christ was born, for without the Resurrection that coming and that birth had failed of its purpose of Redemption. They who make this announcement to mankind that Christ is risen are they who speak for justice, hope, truth, and righteousness; and only the Church, only the followers of Christ, make this proclamation. Science does not make it; art does not make it; literature does not make it; business does not make it; the Church alone proclaims it.

The second way in which the women reached their conclusion was by the testimony of their senses and their reason. The angels not only told them that Christ was risen, but invited them to certify to the fact themselves. "Come, see the place where the Lord lay." The evidence for the empty tomb is just as good today as when Mary of Magdala and the other Mary looked into it, or when Peter and John, who had run to the tomb afterward, entered in and saw the napkin folded and the graveclothes lying, and believed.

There was no doubt about the empty grave. The question then is, How does it come to be empty? Where was the body? for the record is, "They found not the body." Where was it?

The first explanation given was that of the scribes and Pharisees who bribed the soldiers on guard at the sepulcher to spread the report that while they were sleeping the disciples came and stole his body. If that were true, then we would have to believe something more difficult than the Resurrection itself. We would have to believe that the moral phenomenon of Christianity and the preaching of the gospel by the Apostles sprang out of fraud and hypocrisy. We would have to believe that with the dead body on their hands, hidden away somewhere, the Apostles went forth with unmeasured enthusiasm and unmeasured courage, ready to suffer persecution and death, for the sake of the gospel, and proclaimed Christ and the Resurrection, knowing it was a lie. That is the most unthinkable thing in the world. The character of the Apostles and the beauty of the four Gospels, and their moral majesty, cannot have come from such a source. A corrupt tree cannot bring forth good fruit.

If the friends of Christ did take his body away, then what about the enemies of Christ? That need not detain us for a moment; for if they had the body on their hands, they would have produced it to prove that the Apostles were liars and impostors when they preached that Christ was risen.

That brings us to another possible, or rather impossible, explanation of the empty grave; that is, that Christ was not really risen and did not appear to the disciples and the women, but they in their grief and in their desire to see Christ began to imagine that they had seen him. Their grief created their visions, and their visions in turn created the belief in the Resurrection. But here again, if the Apostles and the friends of Jesus were only hallucinated and deceived visionaries, their preaching and the spread of the Gospel could easily have been stopped and frustrated by the enemies of Christ. All they had to do was to take the body out of the grave and show that the whole thing was an empty hallucination. But this was never done. "They found not the body." Every theory of the belief in the Resurrection, except the theory of the angels, "He is not here: for he is risen," is broken and shattered on that empty tomb. The only explanation of the empty tomb and the great belief in the Resurrection is the *fact* of the Resurrection.

II. The Meaning and the Power of the Fact

The fact and the belief in it created Christianity. There can be no doubt as to that. Even the enemies of the Gospel, although they tried to disprove the fact, have never denied that it was *belief in the fact* which created the Church and sent the gospel throughout the world. The empty tomb was the cradle of the Church. The first disciples, we are told, preached Jesus *and* the Resurrection. Can you imagine them preaching Jesus without the Resurrection? Some, indeed, seem to try to do that today. They speak of the abiding spirit and persisting personality of Jesus. But what a Jesus! You could not say that the birth of Jesus created the Church, nor could you say that the death of Jesus on the Cross created the Church, sublime and central as those facts are. But we do say that the Resurrection of Christ created the Church. The belief in it transformed a small group of grieving women and discouraged, despondent men into the moral and spiritual heroes who went forth to preach Jesus and the Resurrection and turn the world upside down.

Why was it that belief in the fact of the Resurrection could work so great a miracle? What was it that this fact of the Resurrection meant, and what does it mean today?

In the first place, it declares that this Jesus who died on the Cross and rose again from the dead is the Son of God. As Paul puts it, in his letter to the Romans, "declared to be the Son of God with power by the resurrection from the dead."

do good, to be good, and to make others
ot be in vain.

"He died!
him perished all that men hold dear;
beside him in the sepulcher,
ew corse cold, and all things beautiful beside
when he died.

He rose!
ith him hope rose, and life and light.
said, 'Not Christ but Death died yesternight.'
joy and truth and all things virtuous
ose when he rose." 2

Author unknown.

Now that we know Christ and put all our trust in him, we might say that his sinless character, his beautiful teachings, his deathless influence, the miracles which he wrought, proclaim him to be the Son of God. But suppose we had all that, without the fact of the Resurrection. It would mean nothing. It was the Resurrection from the dead that put the seal of truth to Christ's claim to be the Son of God. We read that after the Resurrection the disciples "worshiped him." They never worshiped him, or tried to worship him, before the Resurrection. But *after* the Resurrection they did worship him; for the Resurrection filled them with awe, and they knew now beyond the peradventure of a doubt that God was in Christ.

Since the Resurrection declared Jesus to be the Son of God, it also declared that his death on the Cross had power to atone for sin. The One who hung on the Cross between the two thieves was none other than the Lamb of God slain from the foundations of the world. Christianity rests upon two things: first of all, what Christ has done; and second, who he was. The value of what he did on the Cross depends upon who it was who died on the Cross.

Once again, the Fact of the Resurrection vindicates all that Christ taught about life, and all that he said about the soul and the life to come. In his *What Is Christianity?* [1] Harnack declares: "Whatever may

[1] Published by G. P. Putnam's Sons.

have happened at the grave, and in the matter of the appearances, one thing is certain: this grave was the birthplace of the indestructible belief that death is vanquished, that there is a Life Eternal. It is useless to cite Plato. It is useless to point to the Persian religion and the ideas on literature of later Judaism. All that would have perished, and has perished; but the certainty of the Resurrection and of a Life Eternal, which is bound up with the grave in Joseph's garden, has not perished; and on the conviction that Jesus lives, we still base those hopes of citizenship in an Eternal City which make our earthly life worth living and tolerable. Wherever, despite all the weight of nature, there is a strong faith in the infinite value of the soul, wherever death has lost its terrors, wherever the sufferings of the present are measured against a future of glory, this feeling of life is bound up with the conviction that Jesus Christ has passed through death, that God has awakened him, and raised him to life and glory."

We miss the full meaning and grandeur of the Resurrection if we make it mean just the fact that there is life after death. It is more than that. It is what that life after death, the fact of it, means, and what interpretation it gives to our life here, as well as hereafter, that is the significance and the power and the glory of the fact of the Resurrection. One who was familiar with the habits and the thought of the ancient world said, "The absence of any cer-

tainty tha
at the heart
of Christ, an
unshakable an
permanent valu
highest within us
that the soul is no

To every concep
earthy, to every vau
would make man just
mal and pagan thought
soul, of human relationsh
destiny, that great announ
is not here: for he is risen,"
them, to all these godless and
of man and his future, "Thou
rupt, thou art damnable!" I
summed all this up in his own g
manner when, at the close of the m
chapter of First Corinthians, the
on immortality ever penned, he said,
that is, because Christ has risen and
robbed of its sting, and the grave robb
tory—"therefore, my beloved brethren,
fast, unmovable, always abounding in the w
Lord, forasmuch as ye know that your labor
vain in the Lord." Because he is not here,
cause he is risen, we know that life has grand
and sublime meaning, and that every effort th

put forth to
good shall n

And with
Hope la
Love gr
Died

And v
Men
And
R

2